WHAT'S A CHAP TO DO?

Anguished Letters to the *Shooting Gazette*

Quiller

WHAT'S A CHAP TO DO?

Anguished Letters to the *Shooting Gazette*

Wise Words from Uncle Giles

First published in the UK in 2014
by Quiller, an imprint of Quiller Publishing Ltd

British Library Cataloguing-in-Publication Data
A catalogue record for this book
is available from the British Library

ISBN 978-1-84689-195-3

Printed in China

Cover illustration by Glenda Steel

Quiller
An imprint of Quiller Publishing Ltd
Wykey House, Wykey, Shrewsbury, SY4 1JA
Tel: 01939 261616, Fax: 01939 261606
E-mail: info@quillerbooks.com
Website: www.quillerpublishing.com

Acknowledgements

My thanks are due to Will Hetherington, Editor of the *Shooting Gazette,* who appointed me to the role of Agony Uncle to his readers several years ago, and to the readers themselves for sharing their concerns with us and a wider public.

I can only hope that the advice offered has put some troubled sporting minds at rest and, perhaps, reassured others who have encountered similar issues.

Giles Catchpole

By the same author:

Birds, Boots & Barrels

Shooting Types

What a Chap Really Wants in Bed

Shooting Types: The Second Barrel

FOREWORD

18 CLIFFORD STREET
LONDON W1S 3RF
TEL: 020-7734 2337
FAX: 020-7287 2097

Growing up in Utah, in a gunmaking family, I was given my first gun at the age of eight, and fairly promptly introduced to the local traditions of shooting. This usually meant waking up before dawn, fitting as many layers as I could underneath my camo, and wading to a duck blind in the northerly reaches of the Great Salt Lake to lay out a decoy pattern and wait. I usually shot with one of my great-grandfather John Moses Browning's favourite inventions, a five-shot semi-automatic shotgun. And, as my father reckoned he didn't need a dog so long as he had me, I did a fair amount of slogging through the mud.

Needless to say, British shooting came as something of a shock – albeit in most ways a pleasant one. Luxury lunch was no longer just sandwiches which we'd miraculously managed to keep free of mud. There were proper dogs, a joy to watch doing what they were bred to do. "Hunting" was the thing with horses. And there were other people, lots of other people, who had their own way of doing things – their own code, as it were – developed over the centuries.

So there were a lot of questions. Some were naïve and easy to get accustomed to once one got the drill. What happened to the rest of my trousers? Sloe gin at elevenses, really? But others were deeper, and more likely to cause a raised eyebrow – or, worse, a pursed lip – if the unstated code were violated. Who do I tip, and how much? What do I do if my neighbour is shooting my birds? Or, if I dare admit it, if I shoot some of his? Which ones really are my birds anyway?

Though no doubt I have raised some eyebrows over the years – and perhaps even pursed a lip or two – I have been most fortunate in having a friend in Giles to guide me through the sporting and social life of the Great British shoot. Giles is a true gentleman in the field and out. He is deeply knowledgeable about the history and traditions of British shooting, to the extent that he can contrast the cigar-holder preferences of the great Victorian shots. He has that rare combination of wit, intellect and humility that can make the best of the past live in the present. His advice always carries a weight far beyond the lightness with which it is given. I am proud to know Giles, and on occasion to shoot alongside him (though when I peer through a fog of gunsmoke towards his peg, I do sometimes wish he would reserve the black powder for windy days).

I'm also proud to recommend this compendium of the wisdom of his avuncular persona, Uncle Giles, gathered from the pages of the better part of a decade's worth of the Shooting Gazette. For those moments when the right way is unclear, and one wonders what a chap ought to do, there is now an answer: read "What's a Chap to Do?". You just may come out a better person. But you will certainly learn, and laugh. What more could a chap reasonably ask?

John Browning

John Browning
September 2013

INTRODUCTION

There are many excellent books to advise the novice shooter on proper gun handling, safety and accuracy. However, no manual can hope to address every problem that might arise in the shooting field or, indeed, beyond it. More particularly, being British, there are many such issues which we would never dream of mentioning, let alone actually discussing. A pursed lip or a raised eyebrow, or even perhaps a spot of throat clearing may be as far as many chaps are prepared to go in addressing some of these important matters. But while these gestures may, indeed, speak volumes they are open to misinterpretation and misunderstanding with possibly disastrous consequences.

When confronted by such a situation – where no one is saying anything but the silence is shrieking volumes – a chap needs a chap to have a bit of a chat with. A few words of advice, a reassuring hand on the shoulder, that just puts a chap's mind at rest and sets him comfortably back on the straight and narrow.

Uncle Giles is such a chap and his wise words have been clarifying these matters for readers of the *Shooting Gazette* for a number of years.

A selection of these concerns – and their resolution – are now shared with a wider public.

Tips for Traps?

Dear Uncle Giles,

When I was a lad my father would, from time to time, take me for a shooting lesson. At the end of the lesson he would pay the instructor and then he would press a ten bob note into the man's hand and say, "That's for the lad on the traps." Should one do this today, I wonder?

BDH, Suffolk

I also recall the same transaction taking place when I was taken to the shooting school as a youth. Mark you, that is four decades gone and the shooting school is a very different place today. The traps are all electronic now and while there is, no doubt, a lad of some sort lugging boxes of clays about hither and yon among the bushes and up the towers, he is no longer straining away at the springs in the way he was in the days of our youth.

I have an appreciation that the nature of tuition has changed irrevocably in the interim. The price of the lesson is clearly set out and the cost of the cartridges and clays and the instructor's time are all included as is the fee for the lad doing the lugging about and, for that matter, the cost of the electricity that powers the traps.

There is, as the consequence, no need for a tip for anyone any more. Times have changed.

Having said which, if you wander about the place pressing 50ps into chaps' hands as you go, you will quickly achieve a reputation as considerably – and possibly endearingly – eccentric. An endearingly skinflint eccentric though, so perhaps you should make it a quid to be on the safe side.

Generosity Obliged

Dear Uncle Giles,

Is a handwritten letter of thanks after a shooting day absolutely essential?

FW, Hampshire

I'm afraid that a handwritten note is pretty much obligatory if you have enjoyed a day as someone's guest. Basically it works like this; shooting is an expensive undertaking and if your host has been kind enough to lavish a gift of very considerable value on you – for whatever reason – then the least, frankly, that you can do in return is to write a decent thank you letter in proper ink and on proper paper. It is a small thing, after all, and certainly takes only little more time than it will take your host to draw a red line through your name in his Game Book. Where your host may very well be looking for something reciprocal (such as a return invitation or some business advantage perhaps) the letter, along the lines of "My dear chap, your kindness knows no bounds and since I have no means by which to return your generosity please accept my deepest thanks etc. etc.", effectively neutralises the obligation and is, accordingly, even more important.

If you have been entertained by an old friend then the informality of an emailed thank you may be acceptable, although personally I am of the view that old friends are, if anything, even more entitled to a proper missive. On a let day where you have been a paying Gun, a brief note of thanks to your host, with a word of recognition for his keepers and other staff, will distinguish you from the mass of paying punters and should ensure that you get the better drives and the good claret if you turn up again next season.

How Long is Too Long?

Dear Uncle Giles,

How long should one spend hunting for a pricked bird at the end of a drive?

TD-S, Leicestershire

Two things to remember here: on the one hand we all, naturally, have an obligation to see that everything we shoot is picked; on the other we owe it to our host and his keepers and beaters, as well as to the other Guns, not to hold up the progress of the whole day for an unconscionably long time. The Gun who has "a long hen with a leg down..." after every drive and insists on plodding across three fields of plough in pursuit of it is soon recognised and quickly exiled from the team. One answer, of course, and the best one, is to kill all your birds thoroughly in the first place so the situation doesn't arise. However, we are none of us perfect, so the thing is to keep searching until your host urges you to rejoin the other Guns. If your dog is at that very instant pointing firmly at a bush, make a last effort there and then do as you are told. You make no mention, I note, of professional pickers-up. In the absence of these, then the foregoing applies.

Where there are teams of dogs behind the line for the purpose make sure that they are fully informed of the gender, species and point of fall of your bird and then leave them to it. It is entirely appropriate then to enquire after their success at some later juncture. If they have duly found it then congratulations and thanks are in order. If they haven't, then a pursed lip and a modest curse are appropriate. Either route marks you out as a sportsman who is properly concerned to retrieve his game and gives you a chance to chat to the pickers-up in any case, which everyone should try to do during the course of the day.

Grounds for Complaint?

Dear Uncle Giles,

Why is it that no one shoots ground game? Or more especially why is it that the shooting of ground game is specifically forbidden on most shoots? We have any number of hares in this part of the country and yet we never shoot them.

PDT, Norfolk

We live in safety conscious times. Actually, Health & Safety Executive conscious times. The shooting of ground game fell into desuetude with the rise in the letting of shooting to paying Guns. Hosts had no idea whether they were remotely safe and erring (quite sensibly in some cases) on the side of caution, and because good beaters are hard to find, insisted visiting shooters focus on feathered game rather than fur; and above head height into the bargain. This saves the inevitable embarrassment of paying guests shooting the staff or, less critically, each other.

In addition it means that there are plenty of hares about for the family days and the annual hare shoot undertaken in February by the keeper and his friends who have a jolly time blazing away at each other's ankles. In hunting and coursing country, of course, it would never do to shoot hares anyway. Now that harriers and coursing are banned this may change, although I doubt it.

RUNNING AGROUND

Dear Uncle Giles,

Is it permissible to shoot a running bird on the ground?

HSD'A, Yorkshire

This is definitely a thorny one. The modern convention for not shooting ground game stems largely from the rise in let shooting where a host has no idea whether the Guns who arrive are even vaguely competent or perhaps downright dangerous. At least by restricting them to things in the air there is a sporting chance of getting beaters and pickers-up home in one piece. Accordingly, shooting runners when you have been specifically told not to shoot ground game – and what else is a pheasant legging it across the plough if not ground game? – is a breach of the rules and likely to attract opprobrium as a consequence.

Where one is among friends, however, or even on a let day where one has visited sufficiently regularly to have some standing with one's host concerning the general safety and demeanour of the team, I would hesitate only long enough to check the precise whereabouts of dogs and pickers-up behind before letting fly. I'm bound to say that you should be pretty confident of knocking over your runner first time though. Turning smartly about on your peg and delivering a necessary coup de grâce before readdressing your front is one thing; standing there blazing away blowing lumps of turf out of the sward while the benighted bird limps and staggers between the craters is quite another.

If it doesn't fall over comprehensively at the first shot therefore, discretion being the better part of valour, wave at the nearest picker-up and point it out and then get on and shoot the next one a bit better.

Double Trouble

Dear Uncle Giles,

I have been invited to shoot at a double-gun day. I only have one gun and I have never shot double-guns before. What steps should I take?

AJT, Leicestershire

What a lovely and generous treat you have been offered. The obvious answer is to rush out and buy a pair of guns from one of our premier London makers and hire a chap forthwith to practise with you for a week or so and then to pass them to you on the day. A cheaper option would be to rush out and buy a pair of more modest guns – say a pair of Silver Pigeons – and practise changing with an instructor at your local shooting school. Then graciously accept the services of a loader provided for you on the day.

On the other hand you could contact your host and explain that you don't have a pair of guns but that you would be happy to have a loader stuff for you while using a single gun – though you should be aware that if the shooting is going to be very busy a single gun will get horribly hot, very quickly, and that a heavy glove and a barrel shield will be essential.

Actually, it isn't essential to use a matched pair of guns on a double-gun day. As long as you have two guns of the same gauge and with which you are equally competent it is reasonable to pitch up with them and just get on with it.

What you should do is have a bit of a practice before the day. Either a friend with some experience or an instructor at your local school will happily spend a little time doing the loading fandango with you, until you are comfortable with the procedure. Remember (if you are right-handed), it is give to the loader on the inside with the right hand, take from the loader on the outside with the left hand. Safety catches on at all times. The biggest difficulty is remembering not to open the gun after firing.

On the day, don't be shy. Have a few practice changes with your loader before you start and take your time when the drive starts. Double guns can be a licence to fire twice as much ammunition for half the accuracy, so the key is to focus on your shooting first and changing guns a slow second. It is unlikely that the volume of birds will be such as to make speed the top priority and a clash of barrels will ruin your day in any case. So take your time and have fun.

That Sinking Feeling

Dear Uncle Giles,

My 4x4 recently got stuck on a shoot. I was at the front of the vehicles. The first drive was held up by about half an hour. I'm wondering if apologies are in order – not that I'm looking for a scapegoat – but isn't the terrain the shoot managers fault?

FP, Wales

We're a bit thin on the facts here and, as a matter of fact 4x4s don't get stuck by themselves, someone has to sink them; which makes me wonder if we have the whole story.

Basically, if you have a truck and you consent – or request – to drive it round the shoot, you imply that you and it together have the ability to cope with whatever the shoot has to offer mud-wise much as set out in the glossy ad in the *Shooting Gazette*. Your host is entitled to take you at your word then as being competent in the limited slip diff., low rev. traction control stakes and while he should not urge you into a swamp he is entitled to expect you to get through the first gate. And not to whine when you sideswipe the passenger door against the gatepost either.

As I say, we're a bit short on the basics here.

Anti-pathy

Dear Uncle Giles,

What happens if antis turn up on a shoot?

DRE, Devon

The first thing to do is to put all the guns away. Three good reasons for this – you don't want some grubby oik grabbing at your shooter and very possibly doing it some serious harm or, if the horror should get your gun from you either driving it barrels first into the ground or shooting you with it; two, with your gun sleeved there is no chance of your being charged with threatening behaviour when the police are called and whole fracas ends up in front of the beak; and three, it relieves the burning temptation to shoot the bugger.

At this juncture rational conversation can safely take place. Actually it is highly unlikely that any kind of rational conversation can or will take place. In the face of torrential abuse, I find that courteous badinage helps to pass the time until the Feds turn up. Gambits such as "Have you come far?" perhaps, or "And what did Santa bring you for Christmas then?" and "Do you find that facial piercings actively improve your love life or is it all in the mind?" will generally wrongfoot the green hair brigade once they have run out of swearwords. Finally you can say "Well, we don't seem to have much in common so I must be off." And start walking back to the farmyard or house where, if you are followed, your pursuers can all be arrested for trespass with intent since they have no right flat to be there.

When it's Over...

Dear Uncle Giles,

If on a shoot and the horn is sounded, is there a grace period that a shot may be fired afterwards? I was on a driven day and a woodcock came over. Admittedly the woodcock was felled after the horn, but it was a rare chance. I didn't think the scornful looks were warranted. Was I really so wrong?

HF, Northumbria

I'm afraid they were and you were. How long would this elastic time of which you speak be? A second? A minute? Ten? Ultimately the key to sportsmanship is courtesy. Your host has outlined the rules for the day and the end of the drive is signalled by a horn. He knew it. You knew it. He thought you knew it. The woodcock obviously knew it and timed his flight accordingly.

To shoot after the horn disobeys your host's instructions and flaunts the fact into the bargain. That is discourteous to him.

To kill the woodcock after the legitimate period for shooting is discourteous to the woodcock; who deserves better. Rare chance it may be but if you cannot raise your hat to a brave and lucky adversary as he passes you in the field then you'll be no sportsman, my son.

Cross Purposes

Dear Uncle Giles,

We are eight Guns standing at our pegs and I am in the middle of the line. It is a bright sunny day and two pheasants, one after the other, are flushed by the beaters and come diagonally towards me, gaining height all the time. I shoot them both but the Gun on my right subsequently makes it known that as the birds were heading directly towards him I should have left them for him. Forgetting for the moment the morals of taking one and leaving the other what is your view?

RG, West London

When standing in a line of Guns your approved area of operation is a gunshot in front of you between 10 o'clock and 2 o'clock and the same behind. If game enters these areas and is a safe and sporting shot – take it. If you kill your bird it is, almost by definition, a proper shot for you. Miss it though and it might reasonably be suggested that you are reaching out beyond your capabilities.

Your grumbling neighbour clearly thinks he is entitled to first shot at everything and should in my view be poached blind fore and aft as the result. If it becomes clear that every bird in the drive is going to follow the same path the decent thing to do is to let a few by for him to miss and then belt them behind him.

A Loaded Question?

Dear Uncle Giles,

I am in the fortunate position of being often invited, mostly by business acquaintances, to shoots, mainly let days, where the quality of the day is measured solely by the size of the bag. I think we, as sportsmen, all agree that this is the wrong attitude. I do not wish to give offence however, since the invitations are sincerely offered. How can I, with elegance and charm, refuse such invitations while at the same time making my views on the matter clear?

REJW, Suffolk

Hmmm. Tricky. Consider this: "A wise man, and a very sporting gentleman, once told me that we are all born with the capacity to kill a certain number of things and when we have shot them we have to stop. Big things, incidentally count more than small things. I don't know why, they just do.

An elephant for example might count as 50, or a great stag might be 10, whereas a wasp might only be 0.0005 of a thing. The point is that when we reach our allotted allowance we will have to stop. Having been fortunate enough to have shot a good deal in my life I am increasingly aware that I am approaching the end of my allotted limit and, enjoying my sport as I do, I find it increasingly important to relish every shot and every moment of the limited pleasure remaining to me. I am therefore drawn more and more to modest days where the opportunity to savour every sporting bird brought to bag at length and leisure is central to my enjoyment. I cannot therefore accept your invitation because I feel that I would be taking advantage of your kindness while not availing myself fully of the abundant chances offered by the outing you propose. Equally, since I no longer feel the need to organise larger days for my friends, who tend to feel the same, I would be unable to offer you an invitation in return that could possibly adequately reciprocate your generosity. I do hope that you understand and that we will have the opportunity to shoot together when our inclinations are more congruently aligned. With sincerest best wishes"

Yes, that would seem to do it.

... In a Pear Tree

Dear Uncle Giles,

On a shoot last season a wounded pheasant settled in a tree behind the Guns. After the horn for the end of the drive all the Guns were reluctant to shoot it. What is the form under the circumstances?

JP, Cumbria

It is a dilemma. No one wants to be accused of shooting after the horn. However our first obligation, as sportsmen, is to our quarry and only next to our fellows. On recognising the situation therefore you should march to a reasonable distance and belt the wounded bird forthwith to minimise any suffering. Word to the wise: load both barrels, just in case; you may be surprised how difficult it is to shoot a sitter. If your host comes up bawling, simply explain that you were finishing a wounded bird. If he continues to bawl, you are on the wrong shoot.

Reciprocal Dilemma

Dear Uncle Giles,

For some years I have had a reciprocal arrangement with a friend whereby he invites me to his shoot and I invite him back to mine. However, in the past couple of seasons I have had rather poor days at his, whereas he has had the benefit of much bigger days at mine. How can I rebalance the situation or do I have to drop him altogether?

AJH, Cambridgeshire

Some friend you are. Does it matter that you have only modest sport at his while he enjoys himself at yours? Or are you counting the cost of this so-called friendship? If you want to ration your friend's pleasure then invite him on a back-end day when the rule is cocks only perhaps. There may be many reasons why his days are leaner than yours including the possibility that he is struggling to make ends meet in which case you are lucky to be invited at all given the sacrifices he is making to entertain you even a little.

On the other hand, if you happen to know that he is loaded beyond the dreams of avarice but is a miserable old skinflint who is milking the arrangement to his manifest advantage then I should drop him like a shot, if I were you.

White with Terror

Dear Uncle Giles,

I've been invited on to a grouse moor this year and I have never shot driven grouse before. Apart from being very excited I am slightly nervous. I've been told that you shouldn't wear anything too pale, like a white checked shirt, as the sun can reflect off it and deter the grouse from flying my way – is this true?

PAJ, Nottinghamshire

Consider this: you are a grouse. You are happily sitting in some nice purple heather, chewing shoots, when a nasty man with a noisy flag hoves into view behind you. You run a few yards and then decide to fly away from him since it is more convenient. Once airborne you are skimming the heather tops scanning the distant horizon when you see a white blob in the distance with another white blob on top of it. Everything else in the vicinity is a melange of greens and browns and mauve and olive drab. "Hmm," you think, "could be a sheep, I suppose but sheep don't float several feet above the ground and are wider, generally speaking, than they are tall. Think I'll give it a bit of a swerve to be on the safe side." Seem sensible to you?

Muted hues are always a good idea, and a brimmed hat will shade your face into the bargain. Grouse may or may not be deterred by your shirt, as a matter of fact, but why take the risk?

Big, Bad Dog

Dear Uncle Giles,

My five-year-old black lab isn't very well behaved at all, I'm afraid. She has been coming out shooting with me for four years now and each year I think she will settle down but no, she still disappears from the peg during a drive and goes off into the woods. Then at the end of the drive her picking-up is erratic to say the least. On a positive note she is friendly and affectionate with all other Guns and dogs.

I will probably shoot 15 driven days this season but am beginning to have doubts about taking her with me as I know the keepers and pickers-up find her annoying. Any suggestions?

PWR, Salop

A man by the age of forty has the face he deserves and I rather think that after five years you have the dog you deserve. There is no point in hoping that your dog will settle down. If it is to become a good dog then it must be trained to do so and I suspect that you have been remiss in this regard. The running in during the drive can be cured by attaching your dog to one of those corkscrew affairs which is as clear a signal of failure as a beacon on your hat, but there you go, and the only solution to poor retrieving at the end of the drive, at the expense of the pickers-up, is not to let her participate.

However, to take a dog shooting and then to deny it the opportunity to express its natural instincts, however uncurbed, seems to me to be unduly harsh on the animal and I think the only proper solution is to leave her at home. You comment that you know keepers and pickers-up find her behaviour annoying. It doesn't do to annoy such people and your invitations will dwindle if you do.

What you have is not a shooting dog but a pet. Companionable and loyal she may be but her place is at your hearth and not in the field.

Sorry.

Driven Shooting

Dear Uncle Giles,

Should you offer the use of your 4x4 on shoots with no communal gun wagon?

FECM, Hampshire

If the shoot has no transport, it may very well be that you are expected to walk. It is, after all, an agreeable enough way to get about. If, on the other hand, your host is wandering about asking how many vehicles the team has at its disposal, then the proper thing to do, of course, is to offer yours.

You should however be prepared to watch a lot of muddy Guns smearing your cream leather interior while someone else's dog chews off your headrests and throws up down the back seat. If these possibilities alarm, you can say that you'd love to help but you have borrowed it from your future father-in-law and you promised to keep it clean because he's going to a funeral in it tomorrow.

Beaten to it

Dear Uncle Giles,

I am a regular Gun on a decent local shoot, here in North Yorkshire, and like many shoots we have a beaters' day at the end of January. This is great as it is a chance for all the people who work hard on the shoot around the year to have some fun from the other side. The only problem is that they expect me to beat, which I am not keen on for a number of reasons – it's too much like hard work and really not my thing there being two of them. How can I get out of it without losing face? Or should I just pull on the waterproofs and get on with it?

JP, N. Yorkshire

My immediate response is pull on the waterproofs and get on with it. Your attitude does you little credit, I'm afraid. Sportsmanship is all about respect. Respect for your quarry, respect for your fellow Guns and respect for those working on your behalf. The beaters have worked hard for your sport, the least you can do is show a bit of willing where theirs is concerned. However, if you really can't face it – and when all is said and done, who wants a grumpy beater meandering about with a face like thunder giving a desultory slap at occasional bushes? – self-preservation dictates that you send over an apologetic note wishing them a great day and thanking them for their efforts through the season, along with a case of beer and £50 so they can hire a couple of willing chaps to beat in your stead. That way they might still allow a few birds to launch in your direction next season as opposed to cementing your reputation as a rude and miserable skinflint.

IMPROPER PIGEONS

Dear Uncle Giles,

I have been on some shoots where we were asked not to have a pop at a pigeon before the first partridge or pheasant, and others where this is not a stipulation. I'm confused – what's the real story?

AJP, Berkshire

It's really quite a simple premise. Some drives are straightforward with topography or some other natural features – or indeed, lack of them – tending to channel the birds directly over the Guns. Others are more complex involving the blanking in of, perhaps, several covers before the main drive can begin.

Holding the birds at this critical point is difficult for the keeper and his beaters and stops. An early shot, as it might be at a passing pigeon, can alarm the game birds and cause them to flush too early or en masse or even in wholly the wrong direction; and the drive is thus spoiled. And the fault lies with the early shooter, does it not? Some drives go wrong by themselves, of course, but if no one has taken the early shot then the blame cannot be laid at the Guns' door at least.

Hence, as a general rule the Guns should not pop off early at passing pigeons because it might mar the greater sport for all as well as frustrating the keeper's carefully orchestrated manoeuvres. Politeness, in the end, dictates therefore that you should allow the keeper time to offer you of his best before tidying up the odd pigeon.

Grouse Guns

Dear Uncle Giles,

I have been invited to shoot driven grouse on a good moor and am understandably excited. However, I only own a fairly standard over-under. Should I borrow a nice English sidelock to make sure I fit in?

PDF, Salop

Certainly not. Firstly, you have been invited – presumably by a chum – and chaps do not invite chums to shoot with them on top moors unless they are confident that they will fit in. Types of gun notwithstanding. Secondly, it matters not a jot what you shoot with but how you shoot that counts. If you shoot safely and courteously you will fit in everywhere. If you shoot well into the bargain, you can fit in anywhere. And you will undoubtedly shoot better with your own gun than with some borrowed thing no matter how posh its provenance. Thirdly, fitting in – as you put it – is less a question of how you look or what you shoot with than how you feel. And you won't feel at ease with a borrowed gun trying to masquerade as someone or something that you are not.

And finally, many top shooters – of grouse and other quarry for that matter – use fairly standard guns of both conformations but some of the best swear by over-and-unders so there is no question of your gun being out of place.

Relax; shoot safely and well and you will be as welcome as anyone. Believe me.

Raining In

Dear Uncle Giles,

Following the CLA's brave decision to cancel the Game Fair, at what point during a sodden day should one call a halt?

PGC, Yorkshire

Always a tricky question – when to pull the plug – and I think that the answer has to be when no one is having, or is likely to have, any fun flat. What we must always remember is that we are supposed to be enjoying ourselves. If everybody is roundly brassed off and miserable then there is no more fun to be had and it is time to go home. It should be a majority consensus decision because there is often a hard case among the party who will want to carry on regardless, in which case he can sit under a tree for the rest of the day and see what happens. And good luck to him.

On let days there is the additional issue of the money, which always looms large and here again consensus is the key. Most sportsmen are reasonable people and some reasonable agreement should be achievable. If it isn't, one side or the other is in the wrong place or the wrong business. Tricky times reveal tricky customers on either side.

As a top tip, I always keep an emergency stash of really – and I mean really – good claret available to dull the pain. An early lunch is never so bad if it is long and lovely.

Big Bore or Small Bore

Dear Uncle Giles,

The Game Fair is imminent and this year I want to get a shotgun for my 13-year-old son who will get the opportunity for a few game days next season. But I don't know whether to go for a smaller bore, perhaps a 28 or a 20, or just take the plunge and get him a 12 bore. What do you advise?

RAC, Worcestershire

Don't buy him a 12 bore whatever you do. I expect that's what you shoot with and why on earth would you want another one of those rattling about the house? The answer is, of course, buy him a 20 bore – or better still a 16 gauge – in over-and-under conformation for choice. Either calibre offers lightness and balance combined with all the killing power he will need for anything but the most extreme of quarries. There are many makes on the market in all price ranges and many of them are delightful. The next consideration is the kid himself. Is he a hulking great brute of a prop forward or is he of slight scrum-half build? If the former he will be able to manage anything up to 30g of shot in his cartridges and that's enough to take on the very best. If he is more diminutive then you will want to provide 24g loads to begin with or perhaps something even lighter, if needs be.

The load content of the cartridge is far more important than the calibre when considering the effect of recoil on a youngster. And the best part is that you can borrow it when the lad is at school or whatever and leave that great smoke pole of a 12 bore in the cupboard.

Tails of Pheasants

Dear Uncle Giles,

I've been invited on a couple of pheasant days this month and even though I know the season officially starts on October 1, I have been told that it's bad form to shoot pheasants before November – is this true?

BJB, Lincolnshire

It is true that the pheasant season starts on October 1st and it is also true that there are those who hold that it is bad form to shoot pheasants before November. This is for two reasons – one valid and one less so. The latter is because a busy shooting chap should be engaged with his invitations to shoot partridges throughout September and October and I suspect that those who profess to disdain early pheasants would like it to be thought that they are among that exclusive group who are still busy at the grouse when the partridge season starts and fully committed to partridges when the pheasants come in.

Having said which, the former reason is because most pheasants will not be in their prime this early in the season. There may be some wild or over-wintered stock and these are sporting birds alright but the bulk of reared stock will be scarcely mature and we don't want to be shooting tailless cheepers as they clamber the hedge, now do we?

So shoot by all means but show a proper discrimination. If it's got a good long tail on it and is going a bit, have at it. If it's round and fluffy and five feet off the floor, then stay your hand. Otherwise it's murder, not sport.

KIDS TODAY

Dear Uncle Giles,

My fourteen-year-old son has been invited to a boys' day on Boxing Day. The invitation asks that he be accompanied throughout by a "responsible adult" – presumably me – but he says that having me hovering about at his shoulder will put him off something chronic. I do think he is safe, actually, and I do see his point but what is the solution?

RJO, Suffolk

Kids today don't know they're born, do they? How old were we before we got a proper invitation to a driven day, eh? On the other hand, the lad is exactly right about having you in the picture. Things you should never attempt to teach blood relatives include shooting, fishing, tennis, golf and driving and about a zillion other subjects but these are central. So what's the answer?

At the draw first thing in the morning, the juniors draw pegs first. After which the responsible adults also draw pegs. Any coincidental blood ties thus formed redraw forthwith until everyone is standing with a comparative stranger. Politeness therefore dictates that Guns listen to what they are told and that responsible adults keep their commentary to themselves.

OR WHAT?

Dear Uncle Giles,

A good friend kindly asks my son and me to his annual fathers and sons day. Unfortunately he also asks someone who is, quite frankly, the most dangerous Shot I have ever encountered. My son and I are agreed that we neither of us want to go because of the possibility of witnessing – or worse, being part of – a ghastly accident. Is there a gentle way of telling my friend the reason for our refusal of his invitation? Or do we simply make up an excuse? Or what?

EGC, Hertfordshire

I think you have to go with 'Or what?', which is complete candour and confronting the situation. It's the least agreeable course of action and the hardest one to take but I think you have to grasp the nettle. There is no gentle way of telling your friend that one of his guests – and also friend – is an accident waiting to happen and lying to a friend – even in an effort not to hurt his feelings – is no way to keep a friend. So you must be candid. He probably already knows but can't bring himself to confront the situation either. Your resolve may stiffen his. And his resolve may mean that the miscreant mends his ways; which is to everybody's benefit. Otherwise someone is going to get seriously hurt which is a disaster. Sorry, no way round it.

Doggone It

Dear Uncle Giles,

I don't care how many professional pickers-up there are on a shoot, I want my dog to pick my birds. Am I wrong?

AML, Gloucestershire

This is a very contentious issue much debated in these pages as well as elsewhere. Modern game shooting is a business. Founded on sport but a business for all that. Expensive to organise and expensive to participate in. And the bag at the end of the day is the basis for the contract between those providing the sport and the Guns. Therefore it is centrally important that all birds shot are picked. It is equally fundamental that birds, either dead or wounded, should be collected quickly and efficiently. That is our obligation to our quarry. Both these objectives are met by ensuring that there are adequate numbers of pickers-up.

Insisting that your dog picks your birds is counterproductive to both these ends. It slows down the process of picking-up and slows down the progress of the day as a whole.

I understand your wish to see your own dog work but you should not expect to be able to do so on a big shoot where there are professional pickers-up in attendance for precisely that purpose. Guns who want their dogs to work to their own birds should choose smaller shoots where their dogs can be a welcome asset in the pick up over the grand battues where there are professionals already on hand to do the job. You might also consider becoming a professional picker-up on the same bigger shoots in your area.

Wild or What?

Dear Uncle Giles,

We have a walkabout rough shoot, which borders two other shoots. One neighbour puts down 1,500-2,000 birds annually and the other, over the hill, puts down fewer. The fellow over the hill says we should put down some birds because the shoot, which puts down 1,500-2,000, is apparently not happy. But we think ours is a wild bird shoot.

Should we put birds down and if so how many? We do get some birds mating and producing chicks.

TF, Derbyshire

Why, I wonder, is it your smaller neighbour who urges you to release birds on his border and suggesting that this is to satisfy your other neighbour? Could it be that he is hoping to benefit indirectly? Step one is to confirm whether your larger neighbour is actually aggrieved. Why not ask him directly? If there is really a problem there, I venture that demonstrating that you are actively encouraging the wild bird population – and not relying on attracting his reared stock for game – will satisfy his misgivings. Point out your traplines and habitat management contributions; your coppicing and hedge management. I also suggest that a spot of diplomatic strategic inviting might not go amiss.

Second Thoughts

Dear Uncle Giles,

A friend organised a day's shooting where the team of Guns only vaguely knew each other. A bird came over which was clearly my neighbour's bird and he missed it. I then turned and shot it behind. At the end of the drive he came over and complained that I should have let him fire his second barrel before I shot. My position was, if he was going to shoot again, that he would have continued swinging through firing well before I could, having firstly taken a moment to assess the situation and then turn, mount and finally fire.

What is your view on the etiquette of this situation? And if you find in favour of the complainant, would your position change if he had pricked the bird with his first barrel?

JHL, Hertfordshire

What is the central purpose of the shooting day? To shoot game. You say that the bird was clearly your neighbour's. He failed to kill it with his shot, you killed it with yours. Where is the sin? If the bird is killable and you kill it with your shot then it is a reasonable shot for you and you are entitled to take it. If you allow another to shoot at it first then that is a courtesy. If he fails to kill it with his shot and you may still kill it, then you may reasonably do so. The second barrel should not be a second chance at a first bird so much as is the first chance at a second. As to the second part of your question: of course, you should always kill a wounded bird before even addressing a further target. Personally, I think you were right in the first place.

Swept Away

Dear Uncle Giles,

I took a let day on a mixed pheasant and partridge day on the day of the Rugby World Cup Final with seven other Guns, some of whom I knew and where some of us had shot before (no agent was involved). The shoot captain who ran the shoot and the whole day collected the bets on the outcome of the number of birds shot. Before the end of the day he had to leave early for an evening engagement, pocketing the cartridge money as he left. It later transpired that I won the sweepstake and despite a number of gentle e-mail reminders including the fact that the money would be donated to a shooting charity there has been no response. I feel let down and aggrieved especially as it was not a cheap day. What should I do now?

JB, Buckinghamshire

I think that what we have here is a case not of "Cock over!" but leg-over. Basically your host would appear to have helped himself to money from all of the Guns, not merely yourself. Your options however are limited. You could call the police, I suppose, but that seems rather extreme. Confrontation will be at least uncomfortable and possibly worse – a bloke who pockets cash with such ease is quite likely to clock you under pressure. Denouncement in public also risks a libel action if circumstances should not be as you suppose. Certainly you and yours should boycott the shoot in future and if asked why, you relate the story as you have written it and conclude that "I might be wrong, I suppose, but I can only assume therefore that the fellow trousered it, so he is clearly not to be trusted. He'll not have another penny off me at any rate."

Hen Forward!

Dear Uncle Giles,

I was shooting on a cocks-only day last January and after elevenses, the cocks being a bit thin on the ground, our host said that we could have one hen each on the next drive. Well, during the next drive a large Rhode Island Red came past me. It was only about eight or ten feet off the ground but it was making good time downwind. What should I have done, do you think?

AJS, Hereford

Interesting question, AJ, and one that bears consideration. It would be easy to answer that it depends how well you know your host – and that is obviously a qualification of any answer I can provide in that you shouldn't embarrass him under any circumstances. So that if the fowl in question has just popped over a fence from its owner's garden within sight of the drive and indeed its owner is pegging out her washing or leaning on the fence in question watching the drive then the proper response must be to leave it be. Equally, if the early morning briefing specifically limited the day's activities to pheasants it would be similarly discourteous to abuse your host's hospitality by trespassing beyond the allowed species.

On the other hand if you were invited, perhaps, to shoot whatever you like as long as it is not ground game and you are not within striking distance of any likely looking residence for a stray chicken then I should pot it by all means and point out to your host that he should be more careful in his choice of words. You should not however be surprised when you are made to take it home or, indeed, when you are presented with a chicken pie for lunch on any future visit. These things have a nasty habit of cutting both ways. That's sport, for you.

Nice Pair

Dear Uncle Giles,

How is a pair of guns defined and what is the significance of owning a pair?

WH, Lincolnshire

A pair of guns – a properly matched pair of guns – are two guns crafted by a gunmaker to exactly the same external specifications. So calibre, length, cast and weight will be, to all intents and purposes, identical. In addition to which the woodwork of stocks and fore-ends should also be carved from the same timber in order that the figure and colour of the stocks are discernibly similar. The guns should be consecutively serial numbered. Other features may vary. Engraving, for example; and internal choke dimensions.

A composed pair of guns is two guns from the same maker which have either been altered in order to resemble one another as exactly as possible or maybe where a second gun has been made to the same specifications to the first but at a later date. A composed pair will not therefore have sequential serial numbers. Three identical guns, incidentally, is a trio. Lord Ripon, the famous Shot, is reported to have once had seven birds dead in the air simultaneously using three guns and two loaders. Using a pair of guns with the assistance of a loader doubles the firepower of a shooter when confronted by a great number of birds and implies, obviously, that the owner often goes to big shoots. On the other hand, for the rest of us, owning a pair of guns means that you have a spare should one break down on you.

Big Trousers

Dear Uncle Giles,

What is the difference, actually, between breeches and plus-fours and is it important?

BD, Dorset

Breeches are where you put the cartridges and plus-fours are trousers. Actually, the real difference is interesting. Both breeches and plus-fours fasten just below the knee but the significant difference is that breeches have no overhang. The plus-fours on the other hand do – four inches of it, to be precise – hence the name. By the same token a plus-six has six inches of overhang and so on.

As a matter of fact there are three styles of plus-fours or knickerbockers. Mountaineers favour a tapered design. The overhang permits plenty of room for the knee when stretching for those edelweiss in the Alps but the taper means that you won't get them tangled in your ice-axe. There are straight ones which fall in a direct line from the hip to the knee which are designed for walking and, hence, golf. And finally the flared style for shooting because since the roll falls outside the boot the rain will run off the tweed and not run down your socks.

Functional and stylish, eh? Is it important? Probably not.

Automatic Response

Dear Uncle Giles,

Is it OK to take my three shot semi-auto on a driven game shoot?

AB, Suffolk

There are two reasons why autos or semi autos have, in the past, not been exactly welcome on formal game shoots. The first is safety. Where traditional guns are in use they can be carried broken so that the other Guns can see that they are unloaded and be comfortable as the result. The second reason is that being a three shot – or in those days perhaps five shot – it was felt that the ability to have several shots at the same bird was unfair on the birds and therefore unsporting. The former reason can be obviated by carrying the now ubiquitous red flag in the breech when the gun is unloaded between drives, just as one would do at the gun club, and the latter issue can be addressed by only loading two cartridges at any time. Or better still to kill all your birds with the first shot; as a gentleman should.

Over-and-unders were once looked down upon at formal shoots and are now not given a second glance, so there is no reason why autos should not be similarly integrated, in my view. Having said all of which, there are still those who feel strongly that the traditional driven shoot should be undertaken with the traditional guns, so perhaps I should qualify my advice by suggesting that you weigh up your fellow guests in advance of the day and equip yourself accordingly. Or if that is not possible, take a spare gun with you just in case there is a red-faced colonel type in the line when you arrive. As a guest you should never cause an issue for other guests however trivial the thing is. That's courtesy.

Ground Down

Dear Uncle Giles,

Why is it that shooting ground game – hares, rabbits and the like, even foxes – is prohibited at most shoots. These are legitimate quarry species, after all, and foxes are the keepers' sworn enemies. So why are we told not to shoot them?

ARJ, Surrey

There are a number of reasons. The first is safety. On commercial shoots the visiting Guns are not necessarily known to the host and keeper and their response to any given situation is therefore uncertain. By restricting the bag to the flying species the shooting is – by and large and all being well – upwards so that there is reduced risk of any dangerous incidents. To encourage shooting at ankle height has obvious risk connotations.

Where hares are common the invitation to shoot them is very often in the gift of the keeper at the after season hare shoots in February. While shooting foxes in hunting country is, even now hunting is banned, a mortal sin. There are also conservation reasons. Brown hares, while common in some areas of the country, are increasingly rare in others and should be spared for that reason. In addition to which the shooting of hares and foxes is actually a specialised business which should be undertaken with heavy loads. Wounding any quarry is to be avoided and a wounded fox or hare is a dreadful sight and a worse sound.

Top Tips

Dear Uncle Giles,

With the new season upon us I wonder what the current form should be for tipping? With rampant inflation and the credit crunch and so forth, things would seem to have changed somewhat. What is your view?

PJA, Lancashire

It's almost certainly true that times have changed but I would maintain that the basic principles of tipping remain the same. If you have had a satisfactory day a tip is in order. If you have had a good day then a generous tip is appropriate. If you have had a fantastic, life-altering day – then I venture a commensurate gratuity is the correct response. I don't think that the size of the bag should necessarily be reflected in your tip though, except where the numbers have exceeded all expectations – as perhaps, on an astonishing grouse day or on any wild bird shoot. I agree that inflation has taken its toll.

Whereas a few years ago I would have advised that a tenner was the basic unit of tipping, I would now offer £20 as being the thing. One for satisfactory, two for good, three for fantastic.

A Bird in the Hand?

Dear Uncle Giles,

Is it ever acceptable for a shoot to add a pegged bird to the bag?

DWP, Powys

I am assuming that you refer to let shooting? Owner proprietors of private shoot can, of course, treat pegged birds as they wish. Some might add them to the bag in order to maintain an accurate record of birds taken on the shoot by whatever means. Others might jot them down under the "Various" column of the game book. On a let day, however, I am of the firm view that pegged birds should not be added to the bag. It may be the case that a beater, whose dog has grabbed a bird during a beat, might drop it into the game cart unnoticed but I consider that shoot staff – keepers, beaters and pickers-up and the game cart manager alike – should be instructed, as a matter of course, to distinguish between shot game and others.

The Guns are paying for the opportunity to shoot a given bag and so birds added to the bag, which have not been shot, should not be knowingly added to that total or the Guns are, in effect, being overcharged. And that can't be right. We all accept occasional lapses and reasonable margins of error either side of the agreed total but shoots where pegged birds are routinely added to the bag and charged for will, and should, find themselves losing return business.

A Christmas Conundrum

Dear Uncle Giles,

My husband and I have been married for over twenty years. He has been shooting since he was a boy and is still just nuts about it. I suspect however that he has everything he needs. What should I get him for Christmas?

ARC (Mrs), West Sussex

It is true that a chap should have everything he needs by the time he is forty. Not perhaps everything he wants though. You make no mention of budget but I'm suspecting that in the present environment a new pair of top-end sixteens is probably off the agenda? And a Range Rover is probably de trop. Coming down the tree somewhat, a new pair of boots is always welcome. Do you know his shoe size? Any of the makes will do but get the smart leather or fur-lined versions. Also stockings are an item that one cannot have too many of. There again they should be high-end. Raw wool, hand spun, hand dyed, hand knitted. Even a tie with pheasants on it will serve. Silk, obviously. And a silk cashmere scarf is a lovely thing. What he will really appreciate though is permission to go shooting more. Happy Christmas.

Sick Feeling

Dear Uncle Giles,

I fell ill the night before a shoot and couldn't arrange a replacement in time. I paid a big deposit. So how do I approach the shoot about a refund – full or partial?

WHB, Lincolnshire

While I have sympathy for your indisposition it is hard to see how you can expect a refund from the shoot. You contracted with them in good faith – and they with you. The fact that you were unable to attend on the due date disadvantages them quite as much as it does you. The taking of a deposit from you insulates the shoot – to some extent – from a total loss. That's why, quite reasonably, they require it. As the consequence, the risk is shared between the shoot and the guest.

I venture that you are extremely unlikely to be able to secure any kind of refund; indeed, it is not unfeasible that the shoot might seek the balance of the contract from yourself.

When paying large sums for expensive shoots it is sensible to insure yourself from cancellation – for whatever reason – with one of the insurers providing such cover. Otherwise the risk is with you.

Sorry.

Caught in the Rigging

Dear Uncle Giles,

At the start of a shoot the other day at which I was a guest, our host offered us a handful of cards to draw for pegs. I couldn't help but notice that I was the only Gun who was given a free draw. All the other Guns were offered a fan of cards with one obviously sticking out and the host's thumb clamped firmly on the rest. He was clearly rigging the draw. Isn't that a bit off?

LRB, Hereford

Of course he was rigging the draw and it isn't necessarily wrong. It is more probably right. First off, if the Guns know one another well there may be long-lasting rivalries and famous vendettas bubbling away. So putting old muckers next to one another in the line makes for plenty of jolly eye-wiping opportunities and associated banter. More importantly, there may be some very good Shots and some less good Guns in the team. To prevent there being wide gaps in the line it is important to ensure that both are spread evenly. As it were A team – B team – A team – B team through the line. This is especially true on a let day where letting birds flood through the line unscathed on a big drive can make achieving the bag more difficult. You should be gratified that you at least got a free draw. The rest of us are seldom so lucky.

Out of Left Field

Dear Uncle Giles,

I am a relatively recent convert to shooting and have been thoroughly enjoying smashing the sporting clays at a local farm shoot in Cumbria. To get me going in the game I purchased an entry level over-and-under, with a strategy in mind to upgrade once my skill had improved and I was comfortable that I really was entering into a hobby that I could appreciate for life. In all honesty my skill is not improving as fast as the addiction has taken hold, but I am now starting to look for a bargain purchase as a next gun.

The query I have is to do with left- and right-handed guns. I have astigmatism in my right eye, rendering it pretty poor for most things, forcing me to shoot left-handed; however I am firmly right-handed, meaning that I tend to do a complicated little juggle after firing to reload. Should I be looking to buy a left-handed gun and improve my dexterity to ease operation, or am I better off continuing on my policy of left-handed shooting with a right-handed gun?

All advice is greatly appreciated.

AR, Bristol

Right-handed but left-eyed is a not uncommon issue and the easiest response is, as you have found, to learn to shoot left-handed. The other option is a cross-eyed stock that curves from the right shoulder to the aiming point of the left eye. Cross-eyed stocks are available – though unusual – and are accordingly costly. Shooting left-handed is probably a better option. However you should shoot with a left-handed gun. Several makers cater for left-handers. At a basic level the cast – or bend – in the stock is designed to bring the aiming point from the left shoulder to the left eye; but there are guns which are wholly designed for southpaws. So the top lever will pull left to open the gun (this will obviate your reloading juggle, for example); the trigger guard will be rolled on the left for better comfort and access and splinter triggers will be left inclined.

On guns with a pistol grip, the chequering and the palm curvature will be carved for better control by the left hand. And so on and so forth. A whizz round the Internet reveals that several makers supply the left-handed market in both o/u and s/s formats, though details of how completely left-handed they are seem sketchy. I venture that a visit to some of the available forums to accumulate some data is the place to start and then down to your local friendly gunsmith for a chat and a satisfactory resolution.

Bully for You

Dear Uncle Giles,

How much banter is too much banter? I don't mind a bit of 'camaraderie' but sometimes my confidence takes a serious knock when my shooting friends go on the attack.

WH, Lincolnshire

This is a wider social issue than merely the shooting field. What you describe, indeed what you are asking me to define, is the fine line between jovial chaffing and downright bullying. And that is a pretty difficult line to draw, not least because it is a subjective analysis. It is the subject of the banter, the receiver, who feels when the line has been crossed; although it must also be said that the deliverer may also have the same perception. In other words, you know when you are being bullied and a bully always knows when a spiteful dig really gets home.

So the issue boils down to this: do you consider that you are really being ragged or bullied? If you are being ragged, and it is uncomfortable, then you should ask your friends to stop. If they are your friends, they will.

If you are being bullied, then your friends – so called – are a bunch of bullies and you should have no more to do with them.

Damn Jam

Dear Uncle Giles,

Last season my gun jammed halfway through a drive, which was frustrating and embarrassing. What is the correct form in this situation?

BDV, Lanark

Frustrating certainly but I don't see why you should have been embarrassed. Even the best guns fail from time to time and it need not be the fault of the owner. What you should not do, however, is drive the thing fore-end deep into the plough with a curse and then stand there swearing at it. That would never do. What you can do is alert your neighbours in the line to your predicament and encourage them to avail themselves of the birds over your peg; if that is their pleasure. After the drive you should explain to your host that it was gun failure that caused you to ignore his pheasants and that no comment on their quality was implied or intended and ask him to pass this message onto his headkeeper. You will be able to reinforce this when you see him at the end of the day. Then you make your way back to your vehicle and fetch the spare gun, which all organised Guns have with them for just such an eventuality.

Should you not have a spare gun for any reason, someone else almost certainly will and will offer to lend it to you in which case you should accept the offer. You may not shoot as well as you do with your own gun but do not whatever you do comment on this or suggest that it is the gun's fault. Shooting less is not as bad as not shooting at all. And a couple of bottles of good claret as a thank you never go amiss either.

Split Personality

Dear Uncle Giles,

Owing to a diary error, I have just realised that I've booked and paid for a day's shooting with my pals up in Scotland in November when I'm supposed to be at my wife's side for the marriage of her best friend in Cornwall. What should I do?

BDR, Staffordshire

You are, to quote the vernacular, buggered. You cannot possibly be in two places – and at opposite ends of the country, to boot – at once; and dodging the better half's best friend's nuptials for a blast with your mates is clearly a capital offence. You could try to sell the day on to another pal, I suppose, but the better thing to do is to offer to give it to a friend. However there is a technique to this, which may even leave you better off. Offer it first to your hardest shooting friends. Since they are hard shooting chaps they will already be busy, they will therefore not be able to accept your generous offer. So sorry. Then offer it to other shooting friends. If they can do it, so be it. If not offer it to the other pals who are attending the shoot as a gift to one of their friends. Ultimately, someone will be able to deputise for you, so the day will not be a total loss. But all the people you have offered it to – and who could not accept your gift – will feel a proper sense of obligation notwithstanding.

Accordingly you should get at least one invitation back. If not this season then next. The chap who ultimately shoots will probably invite you somewhere. One or more of those who could not accept will probably invite you to something too. So you should end up in credit. And don't forget to underline your sacrifice to the wife and to her best friend and to her best friend's husband too, for that matter. He might be a sporting chap too, after all, and who knows what means he might use to manifest his appreciation of your noble gesture?

Double Troublesome

Dear Uncle Giles,

Can a chap double-gun when he feels like it? There may be a lot of birds getting through – and that would be a waste, wouldn't it?

WH, Salop

Certainly not. First of all, you are not there to kill as many birds as possible but to shoot the most sporting birds you can. Secondly, the reason there are a lot of birds is because your host and his keeper have a whole season to get through, not just today. Thirdly, it would be astonishingly rude to the other guests if you hauled out twice the artillery. Even using a spouse or partner as a stuffer on busy drives is on the cusp and guidance from your host should be sought.

Your invitation will specify how many guns may be used.

There is an argument for only ever using double-guns at pheasants when you are really trying to clear up the cocks after Christmas.

Blackballs

Dear Uncle Giles,

Under what circumstances would a shoot be completely within its rights to ban a gun/beater/picker-up/guest for life – and even encourage other shoots to do the same?

AHP, Yorkshire

I have thought long and hard about this because, I venture, it is an issue fraught with possibilities in these litigious times. Let us start with beaters and pickers-up. Where such folk are employees of the shoot – whether temporary or permanent – then their dismissal, actual or constructive, may, or more probably will, fall under sundry statutes and directives, both local and European, concerning employment. With all that implies. At the heart of these rules lies the question of reasonableness and I will return to this in due course.

Where the question is applied to Guns it falls into two parts. Where the shoot is entirely private and the Guns invited guests, the host is entirely free to send a Gun home for whatever reason he sees fit. That is his privilege.

To encourage others to do the same, however, falls under the rules of libel and defamation the central defence to which is whether the assertion applied to the complainant is justified. If the allegation is arguably true, then no defamation can be claimed and other shoots may form their decision accordingly. If the allegation is demonstrated to be untrue then it is libellous and the defendant will be liable for damages in proportion to the scale of the slur.

Where the Gun is a paying guest all of the above also applies but there is a contractual element to be considered also.

Space inhibits me from exploring the legal details more fully but to return to the question of reasonableness which overlays the whole area: what is a reasonable ground for such dismissal?

My view is that discourtesy is a reasonable ground. The shooting field is a place of pleasure and everyone's enjoyment will be shattered by rudeness. And rudeness is an absolute thing. Shooting at people is completely rude, obviously. Any dangerous behaviour whether with a gun or not– such as wandering off station or putting others at risk by popping up out of hedges unexpectedly – is equally unforgivable. Abusing people is rude. Bringing mad dogs is rude. Shooting, beating or picking-up while drunk is rude. Rudeness is rude. You know it and I know you know it. And you recognise it where you see it. And it isn't allowed, is it?

A Salty Problem

Dear Uncle Giles,

The first drive on my pheasant shoot is next to the sea shore. While most pegs on the drive are well inland, one is positioned close to the waterfront. Does the person on the shore line peg have to use non-toxic shot even though there is no wildfowl on the shoot?

AHT, Cornwall

The law on this point is, at one and the same time, clear and obscure. It is the case that the use of lead shot on the foreshore and over wetland areas is banned and non-toxic shot must be used. However, the foreshore means that area below the high water mark, or more specifically the area between the mean high water mark and the mean low water mark. Which make the foreshore a fixed place but where you are standing, dependent on the current state and size of the tides, variable. It is also the case that if you are shooting game species other than wildfowl and shooting them exclusively inland then you can use lead shot though if any of that shot falls into salt water you are committing an offence. It is further the case that much of our coastline is designated as Sites of Special Scientific Interest (SSSIs) and the use of lead shot over SSSIs is also banned.

So the upshot, if that is not an unfortunate term, is that if you are standing on the beach then you are, on the balance of probabilities at least, obliged to use non-toxic shot. And that is my firm advice. The ban on lead shot in these areas is unequivocal and DEFRA and other groups continue a programme of checks on game and fowl in gamedealers and on shoots, so if you do not use non-toxic shot in these circumstances you are dicing with hefty fines and dropping your gamedealer in the poo into the bargain. In addition to which, if the partial ban of lead shot is demonstrated to be flouted, then lead will be banned from cartridge manufacture altogether and then we will all be up a really deep creek without not only a paddle but also the canoe.

So play it safe.

A Loaf of Bread, A Jug of Wine...

Dear Uncle Giles,

As a guest, should one contribute to lunch perhaps, or to elevenses? A bottle of wine? A flask? Whatever?

TM, Gloucestershire

It all depends on the style of the shoot and, indeed, the style of your host. If the whole day is poshed up to the nines with Range Rovers at dawn and liveried loaders then your bottle of chewy claret is going to look pretty redundant. If it is a pie and a pint on a bale in a barn then you have something to offer.

When responding to an invitation, just ask if you can contribute anything. If your host says "No. No." then the usual bottle of malt and flowers for your hostess are in order. If he says, "Actually, you might throw in a bottle of that cracking plum brandy you had last year.", you have your answer.

Techniques for Tips

Dear Uncle Giles,

When we leave tips in restaurants everything is overt so why is tipping the keeper still an almost clandestine exercise? What is it we are trying to hide in our hushed tones?

PWC, Somerset

It is not that we are trying to hide anything but rather that we are seeking a certain becoming discretion in our personal reward of the keeper for his efforts during the day.

Tipping was once a perfectly straightforward exercise. You had a good day and you pressed a guinea into the keeper's hand in appreciation as you collected your birds and departed for home. Or, if you had not had such a good day, of course, you might not. Or not to the same extent anyhow.

And hence a certain discretion was appropriate. It was also appropriate because whereas a rich chap might press several guineas into the keeper's hand, a less wealthy guest might only manage a couple of pounds. It may be that the generosity of the poorer guest was proportionately far greater than the rich bloke's but no one would wish the details of what is a purely individual gesture to be broadcast to the wider public.

It is true that in restaurants and elsewhere this personal addition to the staff wages has been formalised and that the use of tipping is no longer a gesture but a requirement. But in shooting we prefer to retain the private nature of the transaction as being a personal moment between a sportsman and the man who provides his sport.

Incidentally, taxi drivers are another group who see the tip as their right rather than a reward for exceptional service. An American friend of mine who has spent many years in this country and does not suffer fools gladly was driven in a cab to his destination by a signally circuitous route. Considering that he was manifestly overcharged for the trip, my pal eschewed any tip. As he crossed the pavement the cabbie called after him, "Oi! Guv! What about a tip?" My friend turned and said, "With high pheasants, the answer is generally speaking more lead."

Grey Area

Dear Uncle Giles,

I mistakenly shot a wild grey partridge on a redlegs-only shoot. I picked up the bird and got it back to my 4x4 without anyone seeing me. Should I own up to the shoot captain? In my defence it was a single grey and I was shooting into the sun.

PJB, Wiltshire

Of course you should own up. Come on, it's not the end of the world. It is not, after all, as if you had shot an owl. That would be tricky. Partridge shooting can be fast and furious. Where there are both English and French birds in a drive, perhaps coming in considerable numbers, it is difficult for even the most experienced Gun to distinguish between them. And doubly so when there is a lowering sun into the bargain.

There may be a nominal fine for such a trespass, perhaps a tenner, and a good deal of leg-pulling as well, but potting an Englishman is not a cardinal sin by any means.

Concealing the fact would, in my view, be a much more serious matter since it is bound to be found out in due course – these things always are – and it implies a lack of candour unbecoming in a sportsman. If a chap can't be trusted over a thing like that, where will it end? Eh?

On a more positive note, you should insist on taking it home at the end of the day because the English eat much better than the French, if you ask me.

Short Commons

Dear Uncle Giles,

My roving syndicate recently went on a pre-paid 150-bird day and we shot only 80 birds at 2.5:1. Needless to say we were not happy – what is our best course of action?

CPR, Buckinghamshire

Overage and underage. Was ever an area more fraught? You don't say whether there were any mitigating factors, of course. Was the weather foul, for example? Were the Guns particularly picky? If you were shooting at 2.5:1 your team are clearly good Shots. Were they ignoring many birds which they considered beneath their accepted level? How did you select the shoot in the first place? Was it through word of mouth, advertisement or some other means? Or were there just not sufficient birds? In which case we should go back to the contract. The well-worded contract states that there should be "the opportunity to shoot 150 head of game." If the birds were not there your team has the right to seek recompense for the shortfall up to and including the full majesty of the law. If the day was booked through an agency then your first port of call will be the agent. This is what agents are for, in my view. Someone to deal with problems just like this. If you booked the day directly with the shoot provider then, I'm afraid, you must confront the provider directly. If he is a reasonable and responsible shoot manager I am sure that he will make an offer which, while it may not involve a complete refund, will alleviate your team's disappointment. Depending on his response you have a limited number of options, which are to swallow the loss; shout and scream; or resort to the law.

Double-Barrelled Sword

Dear Uncle Giles,

I recently visited a shoot in a non-shooting capacity but on arrival was asked if I would like to shoot and a gun could be provided. Of course I said yes but it quickly became apparent that the gun was completely wrong for me. The stock was far too short and I am not used to shooting a side-by-side. After a couple of drives of embarrassment I decided that discretion was the better part of valour and explained I would be happier observing. Was I right?

PDW, Sussex

This is obviously a tricky circumstance. A wonderfully generous gesture has turned out to be a two-edged sword. Let us go back to the twin principles of our sport, which are respect and pleasure. Respect for our quarry, our hosts and fellow guests and the keepers and beaters whose efforts provide our sport. And the pleasure of providing and partaking in a wonderful day of sport. If you consider these principles you will see at once that your decision was correct. The offer of a gun was, as I say, a generous one; but since the gun was unsuited to you – or perhaps you were unsuited to the gun – the outcome was unsatisfactory.

You couldn't hit anything. This breaches both of the principles stated above. No true sportsman wants to wound his quarry. Knowingly wounding birds is to disrespect the game. Failing to address the highest and fastest of the birds on offer is to do less than justice to the efforts of the keepers and beaters and is disrespectful to them. Shooting badly undermines and dilutes whatever pleasure you might have gained from continuing, and your disappointment would be reflected in your host's unhappiness at seeing you struggle. Best knock it on the head right there, then. Which you did.

What you should do though, is still to tip the keeper at the end of the day. Not perhaps at the same rate as the other Guns who enjoyed a full day but a gesture of your gratitude for being allowed to try. With a little comment perhaps, wryly put, as to the risks associated with not looking free equines in the oral aperture.

Packing Off Pickers-Up

Dear Uncle Giles,

A picker-up is too close to my peg, can I tell them to shoo? I want to work my dog in the vicinity. I don't have to wait and inform the captain do I?

PK, Dorset

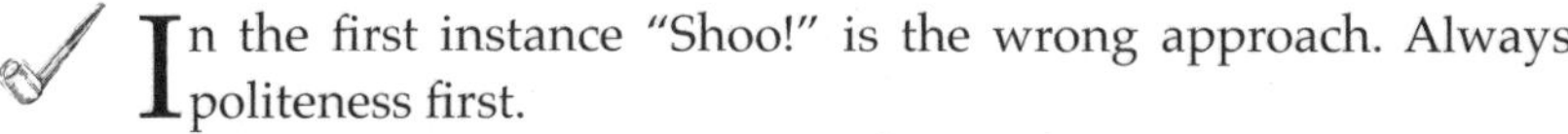

In the first instance "Shoo!" is the wrong approach. Always politeness first.

Initially, "My dog will see to any dead pheasants in front or behind me, thank you. Please confine your efforts to any wounded or pricked birds well back in the unlikely event there are any." If this doesn't seem to get through, "Please confine your activities to wounded birds only. My dog is here to help me and not to be frustrated by you."

If this doesn't work the picker-up in question is spoiling your day. And that's rude. Therefore, "Shoo!" Or what you will.

And no, you don't have to tell anyone.

High Cocks, Higher Hens

Dear Uncle Giles,

A friend of mine is adamant that hen pheasants taste better than cock birds but I am not so sure – what do you think?

REJ, Dorset

A wholly unscientific straw poll among sundry shooters and game consumers of my acquaintance shows that this is a commonly held view. Upon closer questioning the general consensus was that this was because the hen pheasant tends to carry a greater amount of fat. A quick bit of research on the brace hanging in my larder suggests that this is the fact although whether the proportion of fat relative to body weight is actually greater than that of the cock would require more accurate analysis.

I have another suggestion though, which is perhaps associated with the fat issue. We do tend to hang our pheasants in pairs. We receive a brace at the end of a day's shooting and we take them home and hang them together. And, crucially, we hang them for the same length of time. Now, the flavour and tenderness of the birds are enhanced by hanging because the process of gradual decomposition relaxes the muscles and breaks down proteins within the flesh. Now, since we hang both birds for the same length of time it stands to reason that the hen – being smaller than the cock – will decompose rather quicker than the male; and therefore the decomposition of the hen will be more advanced by the time we come to eat the pair and that the flavour of the hen will be, accordingly, more enhanced as the consequence, leading to the suggestion that hens are more flavoursome than cocks.

There is the making of an interesting experiment – and, possibly, some correspondence – here. Perhaps we should try hanging our next couple of brace cock by cock and hen with hen. Then leave the cock birds to hang for a day or so longer than the hen birds – depending on the weather, obviously – and then prepare together one of each and compare and contrast the flavours and report on the results.

Over to you, readers.

Keeper-Free Zone

Dear Uncle Giles,

We were a young team of Guns on a commercial shoot in Devon. The owner of the shoot ran the day. There was no keeper or assistant in evidence.

The day was fine but what we wondered was whether, in the absence of any staff, we should have tipped the landowner at the end of the day?

DBR, Devon

This is an interesting situation and a very good question. I have asked about and the view amongst those whose opinion I value is that the tips that would have been given to the keeper under other circumstances should be given to the landowner with the express instruction that they should be divided equally among the beaters who have manifestly managed themselves on the drives and have provided you with your day's sport.

Cold or Wet?

Dear Uncle Giles,

After the great amount of snow this season I can't decide whether I would rather shoot in snow or rain – what do you think?

SRP, Cumbria

Here's a thing; shooting in a snowy landscape is, I think, just sublime. Crunching across a freshly covered meadow to your peg, with your breath hanging in the frosty air and a tingle in the fingertips is absolutely wonderful. Many keepers dislike it because the birds can be dazzled by the white and not fly as well as they might; but, for a traditional Gun, surely it is hard to beat? Having said that, too much snow can be a disaster. There were several shoots cancelled in the peak of the recent freeze because of the dangers to beaters and Guns alike on steep terrain covered in heavy falls. And not just on steep terrain either. All sorts of things, from ditches and fences to lakes and pits, can be hidden by drifts. And shooting in a blizzard is next to impossible. You can hardly see your neighbours, let alone stops, beaters and pickers-up. There danger lurks and dangerous shooting is not fun and not sensible. And the birds definitely don't like it either. Then again, shooting in rain is pretty much completely miserable. Visibility is poor – with everything that implies – guns and triggers and safety catches are slippery and the game dealer will not be too happy with a bag of sodden pheasants. It's not impossible though and in many cases one has to plough on. I have to say that I shot through several wet days in this last season, more than I have for many seasons.

Which would I rather? I'd rather not; but if you must press me, I suppose I'd have to say rain because heavy rain is at least possible while heavy snow really isn't.

Well Intentioned or Well Paid?

Dear Uncle Giles,

Is a friend's shooting advice just as valuable as that of a professional instructor?

AHD, Gloucestershire

Would you let your friend service your car? Would you let your friend plumb in your boiler? Would you let your friend take out your appendix? Of course not. The key word here is professional. Professional shooting instructors are just that – professionals; with many years of experience and even, these days, training. So naturally their advice will be top of the tree and accordingly of more value than that of a friend, however well intentioned.

This is not to say though that a friend's advice has no value at all. Experienced Shots are likely to have gained some wisdom over the years and that has value certainly, and a friend with some understanding of the sport may have the occasional useful remark for you.

Indeed a friend standing behind you at the practice ground may very well be able to identify successfully where you are missing and a good loader can very often see your shot as it whizzes into the wide blue yonder and that is enormously valuable. But for corrective advice nothing, in my view, beats the professional touch.

Beside-by-Side Himself

Dear Uncle Giles,

For as long as I've been shooting I've wanted to own the beautiful side-by-side that currently resides with a shooting 'acquaintance'. It's now on the market. Sadly, the only way I can afford it is to forego over half of my shooting next season. I'm part of a farm shoot which relies on its members. What should I do?

JHP, West Kent

I am often asked whether expensive game guns are better than more modest tools. The answer is "No". There is a basic price for game guns and everything above that is basically vanity. Will pandering to your vanity at the expense of your shooting – and your shooting friends – satisfy you in the long run? I thought not. What shall it profit a man if he hath the whole world and no mates? As the good book almost has it. On the other hand, my heart bleeds for you. There is something about a beautiful gun that enhances every shot you take. And a beautiful gun that you have yearned for over the years being so close that you can almost smell it must be close to agony. What to do?

Sacrifice is the only answer. Overtime? Sell something else? Re-mortgage? There must be a way round this. How about a smaller car? How about no car? Choosing between the gun of your dreams and being able to shoot with it among friends is just beating yourself up. Come on, JP, it's time to get creative.

Mentioned in Dispatches

Dear Uncle Giles,

What is the correct way to dispatch a bird?

KSM, Nottinghamshire

The proper way to dispatch a bird is with the first barrel between forty and fifty yards out in front of your peg at 45°; weight nicely on the front foot, straight left arm, best beloved gasping in admiration a couple of steps behind and the dog watching the resulting plummet in keen and alert anticipation but without a trace of movement. What I suspect you are referring to is a wounded bird; as it might be one dropped into your vicinity by a neighbouring Gun perhaps? Many pickers-up – who do this a lot – carry a very neat tool, much like a pair of pliers, which quickly and easily disrupt the spinal cord. Since most Guns don't carry these, I think the best way is a sharp rap on the back of the bonce with a stick. Or better still a priest. The weighted staghorn blackjack that you take fishing is the very thing. Or the heel of a claspknife if you carry one. A shooting stick will serve.

Partridges can be dealt with by pressure on the cranium with your thumb. Pheasants, however, are too tough for this method. If you don't have a stick or a priest to hand then it is possible to dislocate the neck. This does not mean whirling the poor thing about by the neck like a sparkler. That way lies messy disaster. The way to do this is to hold the bird so it is facing you and then to turn it sharply about-face while flopping the body over the bird's own shoulder. Much the same action as if you were emptying a saucepan. You may need to do it more than once but don't – please – overdo it.

Short 'n' Sweet?

Dear Uncle Giles,

Is it ever acceptable to shoot driven game in the UK while wearing shorts?

DS McG, Kelso

When shooting walked up grouse in Scotland it is perfectly acceptable – indeed it is right and proper – to wear a kilt. It is comfortable and convenient and ineffably stylish. You don't even have to be a Scot. You should not wear a clan tartan, of course, but kilts come in plain weaves as well as plaid. And if you can wear a kilt to shoot walking up, then why not for driven grouse too? Exactly. Now if you can shoot grouse in a kilt, then why not September partridges in shorts? There are shorts and shorts however. When I was a lad on summer holidays at the seaside, Grandpa would set out to the beach in a spectacular pair of KG Vs. These were the shorts in which the 8th Army saw off the Afrika Korps in North Africa in WW II, the shorts of the Desert Rats; combined with a decent pair of boots and proper stockings, shorts like these should be not only welcome on the smartest of partridge shoots on a balmy day but generally admired. A pair of cut off jeans would, on the other hand, be quite properly looked at askance. As would colourful Bermudas. Or hot pants. Unless you have the figure for them which most chaps don't, but some lady Shots certainly do. When you boil it down to fat it is a question of respect. Respect for your host, for his keepers and for the birds. Shooting dress should be functional and smart. It should not distract other Guns from their proper enjoyment of the shooting, nor attract comment from anyone. And most particularly it should not frighten the birds. So, before you commit to shorts, perhaps you should check with a trusted and candid friend on the quality of your knees?

No Smoke Without Fire

Dear Uncle Giles,

Is it uncouth to smoke while shooting?

PDA, Dorset

There is a photograph in Jonathan Ruffer's excellent tome *The Big Shots* of Lord Ripon shooting at Wilton with three guns, two loaders and a large cigar clamped in a holder between gritted teeth. Better still, the holder curves out to the left in order to avoid inadvertent contact with the trigger hand with inevitable disastrous consequence for his lordship's accuracy and, indeed, the stogie itself. How couth is that? A shooting cigar holder? I went to Alfred Dunhill in London once and asked them for a shooting cigar holder and they just looked at me blankly. Which I thought was rather poor, actually.

Was it King George V who said, "If you are having a bad drive and shooting poorly, put up your guns, sit on your shooting stick and smoke a cigarette and just watch how they fly for a while. Then stand up and shoot the next one." Not bad advice at all. Then, as now. Though how many drives, these days, last long enough to be able to ignore the birds for the time it takes to finish a tab. But you get the point.

Nowadays, smoking is widely disapproved of and banned in many places; but we shooters are shockingly politically incorrect at the best of times and if you can't enjoy one wholly improper pleasure while indulging in another, then when can you? Mark you, interrupting a big drive with a seizure occasioned by falling backwards off your shooting stick while going for a high bird and swallowing your Cohiba is scarcely going to win friends and influence people.

Is it couth? Certainly. Is it cool? That depends.

Come Dine With Me

Dear Uncle Giles,

How can I encourage a shooting friend of mine to eat what he shoots?

DGS, Powys

Well, you could lock him in the cellar for a couple of weeks and then slip a cold roast partridge through the door and see how he takes to it. That may be a bit of an extreme approach, however. Though not unjustified. We should all of us eat what we shoot. Not necessarily all of it, obviously, but everything we shoot should be eaten, otherwise there can be no justification for the whole thing really.

Invite him to join you for a meal of game. At home or out. Some of the best game cooks are resident at the great London hotels, of course. The Savoy Grill, Claridges, The Berkeley spring to mind, or Rules in Maiden Lane; any or either will present your friend with dishes to tickle the most jaded or sceptical palate. There is no reason to suppose, however, that there isn't a perfectly good pub or restaurant in your vicinity which will be fully capable of challenging any of those in the taste stakes and at a fraction of the price. And think of the fun you could have finding out? Or entertain him at home. Game cookery is not difficult. Keep it simple, keep it traditional and team it up with a blistering claret and you can't go wrong. If in doubt get yourself any one of the excellent game cookery books which are available and follow the recipes therein. And as your friend smacks his lips and congratulates you on a fabulous meal, hand him the book and announce that you and others will be dropping round at his place in a few days to see how he's getting on. And again the following week.

SIMULATED TIPPING

Dear Uncle Giles,

Is it appropriate to tip on a simulated game day? And, if so, who?

AJBG, Norfolk

When tipping on a driven day what one is seeking to do is not merely to reward the keeper for the pleasures most recently enjoyed but also as an appreciation for all the effort that he has applied during the rest of the year which has contributed to the day but which remains unseen. Though, crucially, not unrecognised.

On a simulated day there is also unseen effort, which should not be taken for granted. There will be a chap out front placing the Guns and blowing whistles and generally managing the day. The Host, if you will. But there will be a bunch of hefty blokes behind the hedge or in the wood or up the hill who are doing sterling work manning the traps. Probably half a dozen; but perhaps more. And they will certainly have done a proper day's work by the time you are done. It takes a deal of muscle to launch a thousand clays and that deserves a drink, I reckon.

So a quick whip-round amongst the Guns at the end of the day is a right and proper thing to do. Give it to the host with a stern injunction that it be distributed between the trappers with the Guns' compliments. It will be appreciated, I assure you.

COLONIAL CRISIS

Dear Uncle Giles,

My gentleman's club has an annual shoot in the nearby Hudson Valley, a "tower shoot' with birds released on a knoll to fly over the guns in surrounding blinds. To add to the fun, one released bird has a ribbon tied to its leg and whoever dispatches that bird wins a pot of money collected from each gun earlier. The amount is insignificant, a few hundred dollars. This year the "money bird" presented itself directly in front of the blind that my wife and I shared and she efficiently killed it, as witnessed by other nearby Guns and by the dog handlers who presented her with the ribbon. At lunch when the pot was to be awarded, an elderly member of the club whose blind had been behind and +50 yards away from ours claimed the prize. After an uncomfortable pause, a club executive offered a first rate claret from the club's cellar as an additional prize to resolve the impasse. The incident was particularly surprising and appalling because the club justifiably prides itself on a genteel membership.

Generally, how does one deal with Guns who claim birds that others have killed and, specifically, how would you have dealt with our situation?

JPC jr, NYC

Since receiving your letter I have been considering how a wit such as Dorothy Parker, perhaps, might have responded to the situation. I suspect she might have thrown the money onto the elderly member's table and snapped, "Take the damned money and buy yourself some manners, why don't you? Or, at your age, maybe just rent 'em." However, I think that, under the circumstances, your club officer trod a superbly diplomatic path, though he might later have left the elderly member alone in a room with a letter of resignation from the club and a loaded revolver. Or perhaps, these days, a one-way rail ticket to Montana.

That great Shot, Lord Ripon, relates encountering a fellow guest at Sandringham hurling dead birds into his neighbour's butt with the assertion, "Take the damned lot! I don't care! Take the lot, damn you!"

I'm inclined to think that this is, actually, the best approach. Though I believe that icy politeness is perhaps better than the intemperate language that Ripon records. If all the other Guns can be recruited to the effort so much the better. So at the end of every drive each Gun should make his, or her, way to the offender's peg or blind and hand their birds to the miscreant with a comment along these lines, "I imagine these are yours too, old boy. Can't imagine anyone else could have got them at that range. Remarkable shooting. Really remarkable."

By the time the offender has carried the entire bag from the first couple of drives to the game-cart, I imagine he will have got the point. And if he doesn't, carry on. He may have the hide of a rhino and all the self-consciousness of a skunk but at least you and the others will be able to laugh about it afterwards and you do get your game carried for you.

Bird Battering

Dear Uncle Giles,

I saw a Gun dispatching a runner in a disrespectful fashion on a shoot day recently. I said nothing at the time and regret doing so. Should I let the matter rest or inform the shoot captain?

MPT, Cambridgeshire

I have said it before and I will reiterate it here: shooting is a sport and, as with all sports, the difference between just doing it and participating properly is the question of respect. If we do not respect our quarry, then we equally disregard our responsibilities to our host, his keepers and beaters and, ultimately, ourselves. And that is not a good place to be. It is always distasteful to see shooters – for they cannot properly be called Guns – beating or stamping creatures to death. A sharp rap on the head with a stick or a quick jerk to dislocate the neck are the acceptable ways to dispatch a bird and if you cannot finish off a hare – should you be so foolish as to shoot at one not being able to do so efficiently – then you have no business being in the field in the first place.

You ought to have remonstrated at once – though it is understandable that you were taken unawares at the time. You should even now raise the issue with the shoot captain who will be able to underline the proper way to do things when he is briefing the Guns – and this other bloke – before the next shoot.

Who Laughs at Bad Jokes?

Dear Uncle Giles,

Is it bad form, even in jest, to ever suggest to fellow Guns that certain members of the line would struggle to afford the day's shooting unless they were a guest of the host?

PLJ, Devon

I can't believe that you are even asking this question. It is so wrong at so many levels. To start with, teasing is wrong. Teasing anything is wrong. There are things you wouldn't tease such as mad dogs, rattlesnakes and Josef Stalin and things you shouldn't tease like anything or anyone else. Quite apart from anything else, it's just plain rude. And as we know the shooting field is no place for rudeness. Furthermore the mere mention of money or the monetary value of the day smacks of a sordid commercialism which, should it ever rear it's ugly head, ought to be quashed at once.

In addition to which, surely the whole point of inviting people to shoot is to display a becoming generosity and an appreciation of the value of true friendship rather than a vulgar calculation based on the costs involved in a day's shooting. Who can know why a chap invites another chap shooting? There may be any number of reasons and any expectation of a reciprocation, whether sporting or in any other form, is, or should be, a very long way down the list.

How would you feel if you made such a comment – even in jest – and the other Gun to whom you made the observation responded thussish, "Why does he get invited? Took a bullet meant for the old boy, that's why. It's never mentioned, of course." Your quip wouldn't look very funny then, would it? No. No. No. No. Never. Ever. I'm shocked.

Wiping the Floor?

Dear Uncle Giles,

When out shooting, if you shoot a bird someone has already missed or when trialling, your dog retrieves a bird that another dog has failed to find, both situations are referred to as 'wiping someone's eye' or an 'eyewipe'. Can anyone explain the origins of these phrases?

WH, Lincolnshire

I have to admit that you have got me centre pattern on this one. I have consulted far and wide and while there are many references to the idiom and explanations as to it's meaning as we sportsmen understand it, there seems to be no certainty – or even any suggestions – as to its origins.

I have a vision in my mind's eye, as I write this, of myself as a little chap complaining to my Granny that I had something in my eye. Her response was to whip out a handkerchief, give it a suck, and to then poke it into my eye and give it a vigorous rubbing. It was not a positive experience, being both painful and demeaning, but it sure wiped my eye and that catches the essence of the phrase being that someone else has to do something for one who cannot manage it for himself.

The Oxford English Dictionary has sporting references going back to 1823 but no explanation of the etymology.

Having been thinking about this for several days I had a germ of a thought developing in the back of my mind. Many of our sporting expressions hark back to middle history and the archers of Agincourt and Crecy. I wondered whether the term "wiping his eye" might not be some reference to the bullseye on an archery target. However, further research suggests that circular targets with "bull's-eyes" did not become commonplace until the advent of rifle shooting competitions.

Nonetheless, I think that it might be possible that matching another's shot in a competition would have the effect of wiping his (bulls) eye off the scoreboard by keeping the scores even, while swiping – in the sense of nicking it from under his nose – his (bulls) eye would, of course, put you ahead of the game. The dates would match, more or less, so I wonder if that is not a possible derivation?

I dare say that some erudite reader of the *Shooting Gazette* will have a better – or more precise – answer in which case I urge you to drop us a line. That would certainly wipe my eye.

FRIVOLITIES BEFORE JOLLIES?

Dear Uncle Giles,

They say it's unhealthy for professional sportsmen to engage in "frivolities" with their WAGs (wives and girlfriends – Ed) in the run-up to a big game because it puts them off their stride. Does the same apply in shooting?

ASC, London W1

Lord Ripon, arguably the greatest game Shot of the Victorian era, used to retire early before a big shoot having consumed no more than a glass of sherry and a light supper. Mark you, he would then practise changing guns with his loader for an hour before turning in for the night. I think this tells us a couple of things. Moderation is always sound advice before an important undertaking and practice makes perfect. No one who has attempted to perform on a shoot – big or small – on the back of three hours' sleep and while nursing a monumental hangover will, I suggest, be inclined to argue with the former while top performers in any sporting arena will testify to the certainty of the latter. Shooting is a physical activity and in order to excel at it you must be physically fit and relaxed in both body and mind. Different shooters have varying techniques to achieve the appropriate combination of bodily strength and mental tranquillity.

I would venture that what you refer to as "frivolities" would not have a seriously deleterious effect on a reasonable Shot's performance; however, I might also suggest that to indulge in such activities to the extent that some premiership footballers are reputed to enjoy on the night before an important shoot would be unlikely to leave you in the best of shape to deal with what will undoubtedly be the best bird of the day.

Head Up or Head Down?

Dear Uncle Giles,

Last season I was berated by an old-timer for carrying dead pheasants by the legs rather than the neck. To be honest I didn't think I was doing anything wrong and still don't know what the problem is. Can you explain?

SEG, Somerset

In addressing the queries raised by readers of this column we come back again and again to what I consider to be the central tenet of game shooting which is the regard in which we hold our quarry and the respect we show to it before, during and after the event. If we treat game birds without this proper esteem then we are mere killers. As a matter of fact, I agree that it is easier to carry a handful of birds by the legs. The trouble is that for this very reason it is the way that chickens and turkeys are carried to market and, indeed, to slaughter. If you think of chickens being offered for sale in the rural markets of Europe or Asia – or anywhere – and you will see smiling farmers with a slack handful of birds in each hand. Obviously, they cannot be carried by the neck because they would be strangled. Our game birds, however, are altogether nobler creatures who have died in a higher cause and they deserve to be handled appropriately. Heads up. This is why your old-timer grumbled and why you should carry your birds that way.

It is worth commenting, however, that game birds are better hung by the feet than by the neck. It spreads the wings, which is better for air circulation and stops the innards compressing against the rear end where the skin is thinnest and the flesh can easily be tainted during the hanging process.

Grouse Grouse

Dear Uncle Giles,

I have been invited on a day's driven grouse shooting this month and it has been assumed that I will require a loader. However, I don't. I am perfectly happy loading for myself and I don't want to be obliged to tip someone I never wanted in the first place. Would it be rude to decline and would it also be doing someone out of a day's work?

HW, Norfolk

This is a prickly little issue and one that arises with increasing frequency these days. The central question is whether the loader – so-called – who has been allotted to you is really a loader, for the purposes of loading for you – either with one gun or two – or, in reality, a minder whose principal role is to ensure that you don't get over-excited at crucial moments and do something daft. Grouse shooting is, as we know, the very acme of sporting endeavour but it also takes place, more or less, at head height and safety is, of course, paramount.

It may indeed be the case that the estate of which you are invited to shoot is required – for its own insurance purposes – to provide minders for visiting Guns, in which case your refusal will put your host and the estate in a difficult position.

I venture that the sensible approach is to make discreet enquiries of your host. Is the loader a requirement or an offer? If it is an offer then you may politely decline it with no harm done; but if it is a requirement then you will either have to bite the bullet and pay up like the gentleman that you undoubtedly are, or you will have to make your excuses and decline the invitation altogether.

...And Counting

Dear Uncle Giles,

In Spain and other European countries commercial shoots charge each Gun for the birds they have personally accounted for on the day. The loaders keep a tally. This always strikes me as very sensible so why don't UK shoots operate the same policy?

DNP, London SW

Let me say first that I agree that this would be a perfectly sensible idea. A chap goes to a commercial shoot in Europe and shoots some stuff. He pays for what he shoots and leaves largely satisfied by his bargain. In this country, on the other hand, the same chap attends a paid-for battue and finds himself between a couple of complete killers who poach him blind and shoot every bird that comes his way. He pays the same as everyone else and leaves feeling hard done by. Probably quite rightly too.

I believe that there are three reasons that we in this country persist in paying for the day as a team. The first is that we tend to shoot in teams – as friends; and the friendship and camaraderie of shooting is a large part of why we do it – and friends should not be so ill-mannered as to enfilade another Gun's birds to the point of rudeness. A spot of eye-wiping, or indeed good-natured poaching, is all part and parcel of the shooting day but it should not descend into unseemly competitiveness or, worse still, unfettered greed. The way a chap shoots will tell you a good deal about him and give you an insight into who your friends really are.

The second reason that we play and pay as a team is, I think, because we desperately want to maintain the fiction that we are not really paying punters at all but the privileged guests of whatever delightful estate we happen to be shooting on. By paying, as we tend to, considerably in advance of the shooting day, the memory of the commercial part of the transaction is dulled by time and we can, for a few hours, forget that the vast acres which spread before us are merely rented for the day and enjoy the shooting all the more for it.

And finally, paying by the bird is, as you rightly point out, the preferred system in Europe. Like driving on the right, or the Euro. And that alone, when all is said and done, should be reason enough for the British not to do it. So there.

Grim and Greedy

Dear Uncle Giles,

One of our regular syndicate Guns has been getting progressively greedier over time. We take let days here and there and with a given target bag there is a clearly allotted share for each participating Gun. Anyone who wilfully exceeds this number is effectively being subsidised by the rest of the team as well as depriving his friends of their share of the sport. What should we do?

IAH, Suffolk

This is a very tricky situation. A syndicate is – or should be – a democratic affair and so the logical solution would be a show of hands over whether the miscreant should be sacked forthwith from the group. However, this may have the effect of causing rancour and dissent in the ranks and even, if the offender is otherwise a popular member, sunder the syndicate altogether; which would be a pity.

I venture that the first step, therefore, should be that the captain should take the opportunity, during the briefing before your next shoot, to remind the participating Guns of their wider social responsibilities relating to numbers and to reinforce the need for a proper restraint. If that does not work – because, for example, one Gun has a hide like a hippo – then the next step is for the Gun with the closest relationship with the offender to have a quiet word. If that doesn't work then the skipper should have a quiet word. And if that does not make the point, a public word is called for; after which the final step is the show of hands as already described.

Greedy shooting is rude – as well as being, at one level, basically dishonest – and, as I never tire of saying, rudeness and dishonesty have no place on the shooting field.

Choked Up

Dear Uncle Giles,

I inherited my guns from my father who had them from his father before him. They are fine guns but they are choked half and full in the right and left barrels respectively. This means that when shooting driven game it is not unusual to prick an approaching bird with the right barrel only to demolish it entirely with the left, tighter, shot.

Why is it that guns are bored tighter in the second barrel and can you suggest any way round the issue?

BWG, Cambridgeshire

The reason that older guns are traditionally bored more open in the right barrel than the left harks back to the days before the driven battue became the standard on a shooting day, when the more gentle art of walking up game over pointers was the accepted way of a gentleman to recreate.

As the birds flushed, the first shot – taken with the right, lightly choked, barrel and the front trigger – would be at the nearer bird, while the second shot – left barrel, tighter choke, rear trigger – would have been taken at longer range.

Once the driven bird had come to dominate the sporting scene, obviously the first shot tends to be taken further out while the second is taken more or less directly over the shooter's head with all the consequences you describe. This is one reason why many modern guns have not only a single selective trigger but also interchangeable chokes, which are a splendid innovation in my view.

The flippant answer would be to advise you to kill your first bird a little later – and a little better – and then to select your second bird from further back in the covey or group. However this is both counter-intuitive and unhelpful.

Or you could make a conscious effort to take your first shot with the second trigger and then to take your second and nearer shot with the open barrel.

A more radical solution would be to bore out the left barrel of your No.1 gun from its present full choke to, say, a quarter or even improved cylinder. Then you would have, arguably, the perfect pair of guns to take your first bird well out, your second overhead and, having changed guns, drop your third behind with the right barrel and the fourth well back with the full choke. How classy is that?

It Won't Get Better if You Pick It

Dear Uncle Giles,

The servants of a shoot always need to remember that it is the Guns' day but the rest of us also want to have fun and satisfaction. On one shoot I pick up as part of a four-man team with its dogs. We always acknowledge that a Gun with a pegged dog will want to exercise his dog and to collect his birds and make allowance in our deployment. However, when a Gun has his parents or friends, with one or two more dogs, who are not part of the picking-up team, but start hoovering up shot birds, dead or runners, it can become a bit demoralising for the pickers-up. I feel it's not quite in the spirit of the day to have these "extras"; although I wouldn't object if the Gun handled the dog himself. Am I being too critical? Another bleat from the pickers-up is when the beaters have done their job and then start trying to pick up and disturb the scent – but I am guilty of this sometimes too.

RCC, Cornwall

PS. I have been shooting sixty years and am now a gamekeeper.

The association between Guns with dogs and the picking-up team can be a fraught one – as the letters page in this very magazine often demonstrates. You are quite right in your premise that it is the Guns' day and therefore they must be given the greatest leeway to manage their dogs before the professionals move in with their, arguably, better-trained retrievers. On the shoots where I attend, the picking-up team start the drive well back from the shooting line.

And by well back I mean a good gunshot at least. The principal job of the picking-up team is to monitor the birds landing behind the drive for those which have been pricked by the Guns but which have not come to ground within eyeshot of the shooting party. The leg down, the staggerer, the cock on set wings that collapses into the firs. These are the proper concern of the pickers-up and should be pursued both during the drive and more diligently after the final horn.

Now when these have been satisfactorily managed the pickers-up can begin to move steadily forward towards where the Guns and their dogs are marauding about behind their pegs. Given that the collection of the long-range fallen should take several minutes at least and the long walk towards the Guns several more, by the time the Guns are within hailing distance they should have had enough time to collect most – if not all – of the birds that they have killed in the environment of their pegs. If they are still mooching about the stubble or the plough looking for something it is possible from this little remove to ask what they are still looking for and whether they would welcome some assistance? Since they will be, by now, under pressure from the host to be moving on to the next drive they should welcome the support you offer and identify what bird or birds they are looking for so that you can carry on the search while they move off. This is the proper division of labour between Guns and the picking-up team. Beaters should not involve themselves with picking-up. It is proper for them to offer to take collected birds from the Guns to the game cart but they should not pick up birds without being asked to do so. A conscientious Gun will have noted the birds he has killed and those which he has hit but which have not fallen behind his peg. He will want them all collected and will not appreciate them being disturbed before he has accounted for them. This is the central issue and no matter how many dogs a Gun, or his party, has they should be left to their own devices until they ask for assistance.

Gone but Not Forgotten?

Dear Uncle Giles,

As a loader on a West Country shoot this conversation arose the other day. On returning from lunch to go to the next drive a tremendous storm was about to arrive with lots of thunder and forked lightning. One of the quick-witted loaders remarked that in the event of the shooter being struck by lightning would it be the done thing for the loader to carry on shooting in his stead?

Could you give some advice?

BL, Exeter

I think that in the event the loader's first response should be to ascertain the state of his Gun. For example, if he is walking round with his hair standing on end and his breeches on fire this suggests that to continue shooting would not only be callous but also dangerous because your shooter is the dictionary definition of a loose cannon. He should certainly be disarmed before any consideration can be given to continuing.

Strangely, lightning strikes seldom leave manifest signs of damage so the decent thing to do will be to see whether he is still functioning. Check for breathing, heartbeat and pulse. Actually, that should be unload the guns and then check for breathing, heartbeat and pulse. If there are no vital signs, CPR should be applied. Apparently, the beat of the Bee Gees '70s disco smash hit 'Staying Alive' is not only the perfect rhythm but also encouraging to the victim. If you are not confident of undertaking this yourself you should engage the assistance of another. This does, of course, leave you free to continue shooting. I admit that I would feel uncomfortable shooting another man's gun under the circumstances. It is a myth that lightning doesn't strike in the same place twice, it just might. In addition, it would be impertinent to shoot without being invited to do so by your host and the other guests. And you would have to tip the keeper for the full day.

So on the whole, I think that a proper restraint should be shown. At least until a formal decision is made by the host.

"This Parrot..." (With Acknowledgements)

Dear Uncle Giles,

If you should have a complaint, do you voice it on the day or put it in writing afterwards?

BJ, Norfolk

If you are a guest then you can have no complaints. If you reasonably feel hard done by on a let day you should make the point at the end of the day and if apologies and recompense are not forthcoming you obviously follow-up afterwards in correspondence.

If someone is shooting dangerously you should bring the matter immediately to your host's attention. If he will not address the issue himself (because the perpetrator is his father-in-law or his boss perhaps) offer to do it yourself. If he refuses, make your excuses and leave.

"All the pheasants ever bred won't repay for one man dead." Especially if it's you. Or are you talking about measles?

Catch a Pheasant by its Tail?

Dear Uncle Giles,

Is there any truth in the assertion that you can catch a pheasant by pouring salt on its tail?

EW, Durham

I'm afraid this is a myth. It's origins are obscure but it seems to derive from the habit of old wives telling their troublesome children – before the days of the PlayStation – that the way to catch a bird was to pour salt on its tail. They would then issue the irksome tykes with a handful of salt and tell them to go and do it. Apparently the children would spend many happy hours attempting to sneak up on sundry birds with the aim of sprinkling the salt on their tails and returning home in triumph. I rather suspect the suggestion that children, then or now, are sufficiently dim to believe such an idea is another old wives' tale but the story was immortalised on the tins of the Cerebos salt company, which inhabited many of the kitchen cupboards of our youth, although, as I recall, the bird in question was a wren.

The fact of the matter is that even if one did disable the take-off ability of a pheasant in such a way it would probably still be able to outrun you or me.

In addition to which, and this was apparently to be learned from the experience giving some purpose to the charade, it is an unassailable truth that if you are close enough to salt a bird's tail you are close enough to grab it in any event which makes the whole salting effort even more redundant.

On the other hand, if you leave a few handfuls of raisins soaked in strong alcohol (moonshine grog or poteen for choice and economy but Navy strength gin will do the trick) just before dusk you can potter back to the vicinity in the dark after the pheasants have gone to roost and find them plummeting out of the trees and lying on their backs looking stupid so you can scoop up a few with ease. Or so I've heard it said.

Getting the Party Started

Dear Uncle Giles,

If no mention is made of when drives begin during the briefing, should a Gun ever assume they can start shooting the moment they get to their peg?

AHP, Wiltshire

The obvious answer is to remember to ask during the briefing. Think through the list of things you need to know before taking your place in the line. How many Guns are we? How many are we moving each drive? Are we shooting ground game? Woodcock? Foxes? Is there a whistle to start or finish? Or a horn?

On the other hand, if everyone forgets to ask and no one tells you specifically, then take a look around; are all the Guns on their pegs? If so, it is reasonable to consider yourself en garde, as it were, and to pot the first game bird that comes your way. Game bird, mark you, don't start blazing away at pigeons. Then confirm the position with your host after the first drive.

Dog in the Manger

Dear Uncle Giles,

We were shooting, the dog and I, the other day and our neighbouring Gun, who also had a retriever with him, permitted his dog to pick up everything that fell in the vicinity regardless of whether he had shot it. My dog sat at my peg throughout the drive and by the time the horn finally went there was nothing precisely for him to collect despite my having had a reasonably busy drive. Both he and I were considerably peeved as the result. What should I have done?

PRW, Norfolk

This is a very difficult situation. It is annoying for a number of reasons. It is irritating because you and your dog have nothing to pick up at the end of the drive which frustrates your dog and renders you empty handed as your neighbour leaves a heap of game on his peg. The letters pages in this very magazine are filled with complaints about pickers-up collecting the bag during the drives, so how much more difficult is it when your neighbour – who should, as a fellow Gun be sympathetic – makes matters worse still.

More damaging by far though, in my opinion, is that his dog's behaviour encourages your dog to run in too which undermines your dog's behaviour and contradicts his proper basic training. Dogs should not run about mid-drive. It disturbs the concentration of fellow Guns and confuses the effective picking-up of dead game afterwards which complicates bag totals and, worse still, means that dead and wounded game may not be collected which is wasteful and morally reprehensible.

What to do? Step one is to ask your neighbour – politely – to restrain his dog because it is upsetting your shooting and your dog.

If he won't, you should ask your captain or host to intervene on your behalf with the same request.

If that doesn't work, the last resort is to call loudly – mid-drive – that you would like him to tether his dog. And continue to do so increasing volume. If he ignores all of these requests then you can only really shoot either the Gun or the dog, probably in that order, I'm afraid – or leave.

Too Picky?

Dear Uncle Giles,

On a shoot day recently my neighbouring Gun was being over-selective and ignored some very good birds. I found this strange and somewhat off-putting. What should I have done?

TWR, Northumberland

I'm afraid that your letter answers your own question. Your suggestion that your neighbour was "over-selective" and ignored "very good birds" is, after all, only your opinion. One man's screamer is another man's pedestrian pheasant and while it does not do for a Gun to eschew his host's birds to the extent that it amounts to a comment upon the quality of the shoot, every guest is entitled to be as selective as he wishes. There are Guns who are fully capable of bringing down even extreme birds regularly and with no great effort. If such a shooter would rather wait until a bird appears that he considers to be a proper challenge for his skills, then that is a matter for him. He may choose to ignore almost every bird on a drive until his moment comes and then to reach up and snatch what is, for him, the bird of the day. It is his decision. He may also, of course, be nursing the most monstrous hangover – or a migraine or even a throbbing toothache – or any other of a plethora of distracting problems which render him disinclined to shoot as hard as you choose to. It bears repeating, it is his decision.
Look on the bright side; if he is not shooting everything in sight – which he may very well be able to do – then there are more "very good birds" for you to involve yourself with.

What should you do? Shoot what gives you pleasure. If he is ignoring birds which you would be happy – even proud – to shoot, then shoot them. If he is happier to leave them then that is his privilege.

Shouldering the Burden

Dear Uncle Giles,

When walking between drives should one's gun-slip and cartridge bag be carried on one shoulder or two? Does it matter which shoulder carries what? And which item should one pick up and put down first to avoid getting in a tangle?

AJBD, Dorset

This is perhaps a more complex question than it first appears. What difference could it possibly make? On level ground, I grant you, it would be precious little but on a sloping or slippery surface – perhaps on a moor or in a steep West Country combe – it could make a very big difference indeed. The gun is the key. Always keep the gun on the downhill side. If your feet should slip out from under you the cartridge bag on your uphill hip will cushion, to some extent, your fall and, more importantly, you will cushion the gun. Slips, incidentally, should always be carried with the stock end upward so that a sudden zip failure or buckle oversight does not deposit the gun butt-first on hard ground with disastrous consequences.

I tend to carry my gun on my right shoulder because, being right-handed, this gives me better and quicker control where fences and stiles are concerned. I also keep my cartridge bag on a loose strap so that I can, as a matter of fact, slip the strap over my head for a longish walk so that it largely looks after itself and doesn't slide off the whole time. I tend to shoulder bag first and gun second but unload in the reverse order. Always get the gun safely down before doing anything else. The best way, of course, of carrying all your kit is to hand it to your loader while you amble from peg to peg with a stick and a pipe.

Distaff Dilemma

Dear Uncle Giles,

The wife of one of our roving syndicate half guns has called me to ask if she could buy her husband a late season day as a birthday present. I am sure that she has no idea what the true cost of a day's shooting actually is and I fear that if she finds out my friend will be in serious trouble. What should I do?

MWN, Staffordshire

This is a poisoned chalice to end all poisoned chalices. If you tell her the real costs involved you risk dropping your friend in some serious trouble. I recall a shooting man who unleashed a cataract of problems when he left an invoice from his syndicate captain lying about in an unguarded moment. And that was only for the 25% deposit.

On the other hand, if you lie – as it might be by cutting the cost in half – then you run the risk of inadvertently subsidising your friend when someone has to make up the difference. And she might perceive it as such good value that she decides to make it a couple of days!

You could tell her that no days are available but she might contact another possible source or, worse still, an agent who will divulge the truth at the drop of a hat and put the proverbial cat among the poults.

The only thing you can do is play for time. Tell her that you will have to check the diaries to see whether there is a spare day available. Then get hold of your friend and pass the problem over to him. He may say that it is high time she realised how much the whole thing costs but it is more likely that he will give you a figure that his wife will accept and offer to make up the difference. Deceit, of course, is no basis for any kind of relationship. Candour in all things. His best course of action is to mention to his wife casually that he has been invited to a big local shoot but that he is going to refuse the offer because – to be honest – he really feels that he has shot quite enough this season and that yet another day would be completely de trops. And, by the way, he has seen a really lovely pullover / boots / hat / claret that he could see making a really handy birthday present, if anyone was asking.

Then again, she might just want him out of the way on a given day in order that she can consummate her clandestine affair with her tennis instructor. In which case you can double the price and have a nice day somewhere yourself with the change.

Torpedoes Away!

Dear Uncle Giles,

In these days of growing restrictions on smoking, is it acceptable for me to enjoy a cigar in the Gun bus, or at elevenses? Am I prohibited because I am in a public place? Or a work place? Or is the whole thing a load of rubbish to be ignored by all right thinking people?

ASH, Essex

The first thing to check is whether there is a clear ban on smoking on the bus. If there is a big sign saying "No Smoking", then this is a clear sign that your host would rather you didn't. If there is no sign, then it is a matter for you and your fellow Guns. Smoking is really quite rare these days, although a number of chaps see the shoot as one of the few remaining places where they can – and do – fire up a major, if occasional, stogie these days.

As a matter of fact, the proper and polite thing to do is to ask your host and hostess and fellow Guns before biting into the Romeo y Julieta, or as it might be, pulling the Punch. Quite apart from anything else you really don't want to have just ignited a massive Cuban only to have to hurl it into the fire after a bit of a "Hem-hem" from the lady of the house.

One generous host of my acquaintance always lobs a couple of boxes of Monte Cristos onto the table at the end of lunch with a firm instruction that the Guns help themselves. Which is nice. But rare these days.

Hammered Home

Dear Uncle Giles,

There has been some correspondence in the Letters pages recently about the attitude of some people taking hammer guns on driven days, indeed, on any days. What is your opinion? And are there any limits to the acceptability of these or any other guns?

ESD, Kent

I am of the view that – and I stress this – *in the right hands* a hammer gun is no more or less of a threat than any other shotgun. A hammerless gun with the safety off is only a trigger pressure away from disaster. A non-auto safety is always a potential threat. Repeaters can still have one out of sight up the spout. Let's be clear, all guns are dangerous but – *in the right hands* – all can be rendered harmless.

I would qualify my view somewhat by saying that I would hesitate to take a hammer gun on a walked up shoot because the chance of a stumble setting off one hammer or other is substantially magnified, whereas on a peg that possibility is correspondingly diminished.

When I take my old hammer gun out on a driven shoot I do not cock the hammers until the birds are in the air above me – at the same moment that I would be putting off the safety on my sidelock. I do not reload one barrel while the other hammer is still cocked. And I never ease the hammers unless the gun is open. And when standing and chatting my gun is open and uncocked for all to see. But these are basic precautions.

I would – and do – happily take a muzzle-loader on some shoots. Among friends, I'm bound to admit – but then when are we not among friends in the shooting field? All right, among closer friends, in case a friend's friend might be discombobulated perhaps. Would I take a flintlock saddle pistol on a shoot? No, but only because I doubt it's legal.

Never let it be forgotten that hammerless guns were widely disapproved of when they were first introduced because chaps could not see whether another chap's gun was cocked or not which was very unsettling for a chap. And unsettling chaps is not the sort of thing a proper chap should do.

Shot Out

Dear Uncle Giles,

What do you do if your cartridges run out during a drive?

BAT, Suffolk

Your cartridges do not run out during a drive. It's not their fault. You run out of cartridges. And what you do, if the pheasants are any good and you were in a bit of a purple patch, is stand and weep. No, you cannot run to your neighbour and beg for a handful more from him. He will very properly tell you to get lost. What you must do after the horn however is apologise to the keeper for seriously underestimating the scale of the drive (and ditto your host) and make a note to fill the other pocket as well next time. If in doubt take the bag with you.

A Lad Who Would a Wooing Go...

Dear Uncle Giles,

What's the form on a beater courting the gamekeeper's daughter? I'm asking on behalf of my nephew who, while smitten, has assured me his intentions are honourable. They get on extremely well when they see one another on a shoot day but her father is not a man to be messed with.

Naturally, my poor nephew is concerned that potential romance may cause unrest on the shoot. Both are in their late teens and the sooner they get together the better as my nephew's pussyfooting is beyond nauseating. Your thoughts?

CRH, Cardigan

"Not oft doth the path of true love run smooth" as the Bard may, or may not, have said. Courting a keeper's daughter is no different to wooing any man's offspring, though I appreciate your nephew's concern because keepers are, as he recognises, usually able to manage matters to their own satisfaction and upset could cause difficulties on the shoot.

Here's a suggestion. The season ends on February 1st and St Valentine's Day – when many a lad may woo a lass – is February 14th. I would advocate forbearance, beyond common politeness obviously, until the season is concluded and then open a closed season campaign upon the lady. If all goes well the situation will be resolved by the start of the next season and if it does not go according to plan, well, by next season it might all be reasonably forgotten and forgiven.

As to technique, I am far from sure that I am in a position to advise but I would point out that spring is always a good season to be walking in woods and wild places as the snowdrops and then the daffodils are coming through and anyone who cannot get things said by bluebell time needs his tongue unknotting.

Oh, and when walking by water, lakes are better than rivers. Walking by a river always requires you to retrace your steps at some point which leads to reconsideration of what has gone before. Walking round a lake, however, allows you to time your proposal just before you get back to the car. If all goes well you can act on her decision forthwith; and if it doesn't you don't have too far to go before being able to make your excuses and leave. I wish them well.

To Pee or Not to Pee?

Dear Uncle Giles,

The house that we often shoot from has, to say the least, antiquated plumbing. A flush sounds not unlike a cavalry charge while the subsequent recharging of the cisterns resembles nothing so much as a trumpet voluntary.

My question is this: is it better, when Nature calls at some unfriendly hour, to flush and risk waking the household with the resulting cacophony; or not to flush and leave the evidence of one's passing, as it were, to confront the next user?

Yours urgently

REC, Ayrshire

Democracy is, in many ways, a wonderful thing. And it is to democracy that we must turn for the answer to this dilemma.

Let us say that the household numbers, perhaps, ten persons – maybe a dozen. A noisy flush, depending on the deafness of your fellow Guns and, to a degree, the amount of claret that they have consumed – which should be balanced, though, by their excitement at the prospect of the sport on the morrow that might be keeping some awake already – will wake some half of the party. While only one will be confronted by your offering. Six to one therefore implies that to keep the disruption to a minimum the answer should be not to flush.

This somewhat Utilitarian view "Better the least disruption of the greatest number and the greatest displeasure for the least number" should be qualified perhaps by the nature of the offering and the, shall we say, substance?

A wee is a small thing while… well, I'm sure you see my point. Or, more particularly, that you'd rather not. So the answer is not to flush. But leave the lid down to indicate that the bowl has been in use.

Your host or shoot captain or, indeed, you, can then do the decent thing and set the old alarm a minute or two earlier than the agreed time and conveniently – no pun intended – launch the cavalry charge shortly before the household is expected to rise in any event.

Dog Collars

Dear Uncle Giles,

Should all working dogs be required to wear collars?

RPS, Gloucestershire

Despite the abolition of the dog licence all dogs are, nonetheless, required to wear a collar bearing their owner's details while in a public place. I dare say that m'learned colleague Peter Glenser may have more specifics on this but a private shoot is not, I think, a public place. Whether that extends to a commercial shoot, I'm less certain, but I would argue that since it is undertaken on private property and that the public are specifically excluded, the term "public place" cannot be properly applied. That being the case I see no reason why dogs should wear collars while they are working.

The reason that dogs don't generally wear collars is because of the risk of getting them caught in close cover, which might result in their being strangled. I have known this happen. A dog of my acquaintance was lost for a considerable time before being discovered down a rabbit hole. Its collar was hooked on a tree root that depended from the roof of the tunnel; and there it would have remained but for a lucky discovery.

My dog's collar is attached only loosely for this very reason, such that there is a sporting chance of it slipping off with relative ease under such circumstances.

Pointers, on the other hand, are often equipped with GPS collars because they can easily be stuck on a point out of sight, just over a crest, for example, and it can be a time-consuming – and worrying – exercise to re-establish contact with them.

Is This Communism?

Dear Uncle Giles,

On four of the shoots I have attended this season the practice has been for the shoot captain to collect the keeper's tips from the Guns and to present them himself as one gratuity. It has always been my understanding that the tip at the end of the day is not merely a financial transaction but an opportunity to express one's personal thanks for the day's efforts and the chance to offer a few words of banter, encouragement and appreciation and to close the day as a social occasion.

The size of one's tip can also be used as a gauge of one's considered opinion of the day.

Perhaps I am even more old-fashioned than I thought but how does one avoid this situation without causing embarrassment to one's shooting colleagues who seem to accept – and even expect – this form of tipping?

KB, Birmingham

I too have noticed the spread of this approach. I am not sure why it has developed. Is it that shoot captains are concerned that their fellow Guns might be scrimping on their tips? Or perhaps going a bit overboard and making the rest of the team look mean by comparison? There is, I admit, a certain logic to collecting up the team's tips but I am inclined to agree with you that the act of tipping the keeper is, and should be, a personal gesture of appreciation or – for that matter, of criticism – for his efforts during the course of the shooting day.

I think that the best way round your problem is that when the shoot captain – or as it sometimes is, in my experience, his delegate – comes to you to request your contribution you should ask him what his expectation is concerning the amount. Agree fulsomely with his suggestion – assuming that you do agree with his suggestion – and then ask if he would mind awfully if you could see the fellow yourself because there are a couple of interesting issues that you would like to pick his brains about or perhaps to confirm that he remembers when you met him at some other estate where he was picking-up or some such small subterfuge.

Your captain cannot in all conscience refuse such a request.

Alternatively, you could always seek the keeper out yourself after the last drive and complete the transaction right away so that when asked for your contribution you can simply say, "My dear fellow, I am most terribly sorry but I caught up with him before we came in. I do hope that's all right, isn't it?"

I would be very surprised if anyone objected, wouldn't you?

Fair Dos

Dear Uncle Giles,

I look forward to the Game Fair every year and usually go on Friday with my wife and children. However I never seem to be able to get around the whole thing and see as much as I want. Should I go for more than one day and if so should I take my wife and children for more than one day too?

TH, Berkshire

The simple answer is – yes. In fact, I should go for all three days. I sense from your letter though that the wife and veg. might take the suggestion askance because they do not share your enthusiasm for things Game Fairish. I can't think why quite because it seems to me that there is something for everyone at the show these days. However, it may be the case that they do not have the need for more than one day whereas you clearly do. You can take a family to the Game Fair but you cannot make them enjoy it; and, incidentally, it is quite an expensive outing if it is not going to be enjoyed. I apprehend that what you are actually asking is how you can get a weekend leave of absence without incurring either marital wrath or issue obligations? The answer is to calculate what it would cost you to take the whole outfit to the show – and I include not only entry fees but also turns on this and that, lunch, tea, assorted treats and bribes and a bunch of shopping by the distaff side. Now double it. Then take what you will be able to spend in two days, unaccompanied by the family, on cute little twenty-bores, new boots, decoys, cartridge belts, gunslips, telescopic sights, fishing rods and so forth and halve it. Add the two sums together and distribute the combined amount between the rest of the family. Tell them to have a good time with it because you're going to the Fair. Okay?

Sporting Breakdown

Dear Uncle Giles,

What is the proper form if your gun should have a malfunction in the middle of the drive?

BD, Lincolnshire

It is rare that a gun conks out completely. Springs and ejectors do go from time to time leaving the shooter with what amounts to a single barrel. You must make the best of what you have and pick your birds and push through a little further in order that you kill effectively first time, as you will have no second chances. You may find your shooting improves.

If your gun breaks down completely you might signal the fact to your neighbouring Guns so they know what is going on and can reach out for your birds if they present a sporting opportunity. Then just sit and watch. You might learn something.

Following the drive you will switch to your No.2 gun. Or if double-gunning, to your No.3. If the spare gun is still at the house either you or your host can send a chap for it. If you don't have a spare gun (and you should) someone who has will lend you his. Effusive thanks are in order and a note afterwards with a bottle of malt.

Shooting Through or Shooting Off?

Dear Uncle Giles,

When shooting through is it rude to leave before the post-shoot meal? If one has a dinner engagement, time is sometimes precious and on top of that eating at 4.00pm is hardly conducive to a good appetite at 7.30pm.

BWC, Staffordshire

I sympathise with your position on this issue. Shooting through and having a late lunch is agreeable enough if you are staying at the house because you can get well stuck in and basically settle in for the night. However, if you have commitments later, as you suggest, it is not possible to indulge to anything like the extent that you might like for the reasons you have already set out. If you don't have later obligations it is still the case that you have to be restrained because you will have to drive shortly; unless you are lucky enough to be driven by a friend or rich enough to merely decant yourself into the back of the barouche and instruct your chauffeur to head for home. And a shoot lunch without a bite or twain of chewy claret scarcely justifies the name.

I think that the answer is to establish the routine when the invitation is issued and point out at this stage that you will have to make tracks before the meal.

If your conflicting arrangement crops up at a later stage then advising your host at the earliest opportunity is the proper approach to avoid possible friction.

I do consider that lunch is best taken in the middle of the day because it allows for a responsible enjoyment and a reasonable interlude before the long drag home at the end of the outing.

Feeling the Beat

Dear Uncle Giles,

I shoot 20 driven days a season on average and my ten-year-old son wants to get involved in game shooting, what is the best way to do this?

KR, Lancashire

First up, let the lad beat. Beating is energetic and fun; and it contributes materially to the day which standing about with Dad manifestly doesn't. Introduce the boy to the keeper at the start of the day and tell him to do whatever the great man says. It is important that he is rewarded appropriately even if you have to slip the keeper the tenner yourself to do this with at the end of the day.

Then plenty of visits to the shooting school. Deliver him into the hands of a sound instructor who will teach both accuracy and safety. Don't try to teach him yourself. You can, on the other hand, help him practise. Parked under a hedge in a hide with a few decoys and a box of cartridges having a go at occasional pigeons is as good a way to learn more safety and some fieldcraft as any, and given time he may actually hit something which can be borne home in triumph.

Then let him stand on shoot days – unless he'd rather beat some more – and watch a friend of yours in action. This is what godparents are for incidentally. He will learn how to behave and he will not be in a position to nag you for a go. "Oh, go on please." Said friend will be able to explain how long it takes and what hoops there are before a chap can take his place in the line without sounding patronising.

More practice, more pigeons, more loading for your pals. This will probably take a couple of seasons but I venture that introducing pre-teens to the formal end of shooting is a deal too soon. The Boxing Day shoot is traditionally when the juniors get to have a go – under proper supervision, naturally. After that, well, it's a matter of what you – and the kid – can afford, although personally I believe that sport should be earned as much as bought. So consider barter arrangements: spectacular exam results – a go at the pheasants, first team colours – get a lash at the duck, expelled for burning down the gym – gun goes back to the shop. You know the sort of thing.

If you spoil him rotten he'll be spoiled and rotten and no one will invite him – or you. Think on't.

Where does Charity Begin and End?

Dear Uncle Giles,

During the spring and summer I have rather taken to simulated game days and charity clay shoots. I just wondered if the normal etiquette applies here? Should the dress be in keeping or are jeans OK? Is one supposed to tip the organiser, after all it is not as if anyone had to rear the clays. Basically should all the normal rules apply?

MJF, Worcestershire

Charity clay shoots are great fun in a good cause and simulated game days are a blast at a fraction of the cost of the real thing as well as being good practice for all aspects of game shooting, including safe shooting in the heat of the moment. Neither, however, is game shooting and therefore different dress and behaviour are appropriate. Your comment about the "normal rules" though reveals all.

The normal rules are courtesy and respect. Politeness is all; in shooting as in life. You do not need to dress in July as you would for a winter covert shoot. You should not, however, look as if you have just been through a hedge or recently finished mud wrestling. Smart-casual is a positive nightmare for chaps, I know, but clean-tidy should be achievable by all. A tie is not necessary, for example. Remember too that you may be shooting more and harder than at any game shoot you have been on, so a waistcoat to protect the shoulder and a glove for the leading hand are important. A hat and protective eyewear are key also to protect against bits of shattered (with luck) clays.

There is no need for a tip, although a warm handshake and congratulations for the organiser will be properly appreciated and a word of thanks and a tenner to the trappers' beer fund is a sound investment. At a charity shoot, of course, robust bidding in the auction should be your sphere for abundant generosity.

Nerves of Steel

Dear Uncle Giles,

I really didn't think the keeper had earned his tip. I coughed up anyway and could see from their faces the other Guns felt the same. In future should I organise a 'group hug' with the other Guns to discuss a suitable tip?

GD, Cambridgeshire

This is always a thorny one and seems to require nerves of steel; but it doesn't really and here's why. Are you ever coming back here? If your host is an old friend then you'll tell him your opinion of his keeper over drinks in the study. That's what old friends are for, after all. If not then will you be shooting here again? I doubt it. Therefore you can tip what you feel the man deserves.

It is a matter between you and him anyway. Unless you do actually do the brave thing and spin him a pound in full view of Guns, beaters and host while ignoring his outstretched hand. If you take this approach then it better have been a lousy day and should not have missed anything you fired at. In which case, damn right.

Late Lunch?

Dear Uncle Giles,

I run a small shoot for friends and family with five or six days a season and we have always stopped for lunch. However there seems to be a growing trend towards shooting through and eating at the end of the day. Should I consider changing the format of our days to shooting through?

LK, Shropshire

A number of issues to consider here. First up, how many drives do you expect to fit in during the day; and while we're about it how long will they last? If you have a total of, say, five drives lasting no more than 30–40 minutes each then you can comfortably amble through them – pausing for elevenses at elevenish – and still be looking at lunch at two or half past. And the light starts to go by three anyway. So you'll have all the drives done in the best of the day.

But what if all your drives are not broadly similar? Do you have two drives perhaps which are major battues? Which you save as your morning closer before lunch and your tour de force after? Now clearly the drives lend themselves to a long morning followed by lunch and a grand finale.

Now let's consider the guests. Are they coming from far and wide or are they mostly local? One of the worries these days is managing the drive home after a convivial lunch. If you have not far to go, it is possible, host's hospitality permitting, to shoot through, have a decent and jolly lunch, linger over coffee for an hour or so and then make one's way home with a clear head and a clear conscience. Those from further afield however may feel the need to set off earlier after shooting stops, so in order to let them enjoy their host's full generosity this implies that fine wine should be served at a midday lunch such that those wishing to make a quicker start have one or more drives in the afternoon during which to dissipate their intake. If all the Guns are staying the weekend, of course, the whole thing is academic. As it would be if you are a temperance shoot.

The answer, if answer there be, is to consider your drives and rank them according to their timings and the keeper's needs where blanking in and so forth are concerned; and then match these with your guests' likely preferences. I don't believe there are any hard and fast rules about this but the principles should be that you manage your day to give your guests good sport first and foremost and a good lunch at some point second.

Giles Catchpole